Difficult People

Difficult People

Barry Winbolt

ISR Publishing
Seaford

First published in 2002 by
The Institute for Social Relations
PO Box 2063, Seaford, East Sussex, BN25 1WA
email: info@isr.org.uk

Reprinted 2005

Cover design: Sarah Demoratti

British Library Cataloguing Publication Data available

ISBN 0-9541686-0-7

Printed by Biddles Ltd., King's Lynn

Contents

Introduction
It's no laughing matter

Other people's difficult behaviour can affect us in many different ways. If we are fortunate, it will simply irritate us, but when it is extreme it can cause more serious problems. When I first started looking at how to cope with difficult people in my consultancy work and then for the first seminar series I was presenting some years ago, I naturally turned to any literature I could find on the subject. There was no shortage of books and articles. Some identified just one kind of behaviour, for example, 'manipulative types' or 'nasty people'. Others were wider ranging, and categorised difficult people under a number of headings, such as 'party poopers', 'gossips' or 'loud bores'. One thing that struck me was that they almost always approached the subject light-heartedly, with cartoon illustrations, quips and anecdotes that illustrated the behaviour, and then recommended steps for dealing with it. They mostly treated their topic in a jocular way, as though other people's difficult behaviour is something that has to be endured, and which, if we have the right tools, we can circumvent or change.

But, as anyone who has had to put up with difficult behaviour knows, it is not funny, and often people won't change. It may be that their discordant behaviour is relatively low-key, such as the simple but repeated avoidance of a task that should be part of their job, or claims that they should be excused certain duties on the grounds that their health is not up to it. At the other end of the spectrum, their behaviour might be viewed as outright intimidation or harassment, illegal in the workplace. Viewed by an observer, such conduct may seem a little bizarre or even comical but when you are on the receiving end, it is anything but. The personal cost in terms of stress and unnecessary investment of time and effort to combat the behaviour is immense. In the workplace both the individuals and the organisation will suffer, though it could be argued (and indeed often is) that it is the inevitable side-effect of people working together and does no real harm as long as it is contained. I shall show just how lame this argument is and how such an excuse has crippling and far-reaching consequences.

In personal relationships the results are more visible, with direct costs which are weakening the structure of our society: the inevitable hardships of failed relationships and divorce, reconstituted families (step-families) and single parents wrestling with the resulting emotional and financial obligations, and generations of children growing up in a fast-changing world. We are barely able to keep pace with the social conditions we are creating for ourselves, and we are doing remarkably little to equip our children with the relationship skills they will need to live harmoniously with their peers.

Sounds gloomy? It is not intended to. I just want to make the point that 'difficult behaviour' – though typically made light of in books such as *Dealing with People you Can't Stand* or *How to Handle Nasty People* and TV programmes like *Neighbours from Hell* and *Airline* – actually causes an incalculable amount of damage which, in some way, affects us all.

When I started to speak to large groups of people at my seminars and trainings, many told me their stories. Some spoke of their successes in dealing with behaviour that had obstructed them as they went about their daily lives; of strategies they had stumbled across to help them deal with it. Others, many more, told me of frustration, injustice, anger, sleepless nights and much, much worse. I heard tales of lives ruined by bullying, emotional blackmail and lies. I met people who told me that they had been forced to leave their job, to move house or end a marriage. I don't remember many laughs in those stories.

Natural resources

In most of these cases people had moved on and were able to recount their stories from a safe distance; they had lived through them, grown, and developed a new perspective. But there were also occasions where I realised that the people telling me their experiences were not so fortunate. I could see and feel their distress; for them there would be no 'quick fix' for dealing with the difficult person in their lives. They were simply so angry, disempowered or worn out by the situation that all the strategies in the world would be useless to them. In this frame of mind, they would never be able to apply them consistently or convincingly.

Most of us, it seems, have the resources we need to deal with the unfair or illegal treatment that some people mete out. Though we may lose our ability to manage for a time – we may feel browbeaten, lost or unable to cope – eventually we find a way through or round the problem. Framed positively, these experiences are part of the educational process of life without which we would not grow and develop. They point to the resilience of human nature and demonstrate that most people get the advice they need from somewhere: friends, colleagues, spiritual beliefs, books like this one or even a therapist.

But there are times when circumstances (or someone else's behaviour) exceed our ability to manage things resourcefully. Contact with the culprit – or sometimes just the thought of it – evokes an emotional response in us which makes it impossible to take control and act assertively. At such times we need to withdraw and restore ourselves before attempting anything else. In short, the people most in need of practical guidance in dealing with another's difficult behaviour are often the least likely to be able to apply it.

Free of injustice

This got me thinking. There was a time in my life when I had problems with people's difficult behaviour myself. I was bullied when I was young, and I have spent sleepless nights, at different stages of my career, worrying about how someone else was behaving towards me and feeling unable to change it. But it doesn't happen any more, so something has changed, and this is a key factor. I started to ask around – friends and colleagues, taxi drivers, nurses, bar staff, therapists, journalists, doctors, managers and their subordinates, students and school children, anyone who would talk to me. Every time I came across someone who seemed to be free of the sorts of injustice caused by others' difficult behaviour, who had a successful marriage or who seemed comfortable in their working environment, I wanted to learn more. How were all these people doing it? How is it, I wondered, that while so many of those I met told me horror stories about the treatment dished out to them in their lives, other people sail through events without having to fight for respect or even their survival, even when, to all appearances, that would seem to be impossible? Of particular interest to me were those people who had overcome difficult behaviour, especially those who I knew had previously been seriously troubled in this way but who now were free of it.

So often, when we have a problem, we turn it over and over in our minds. We look at it in ever greater detail as though, if we look hard enough, the solution will jump out at us. Worse, often we may turn to 'experts' who do the same, unable to offer much in the way of practical help or guidance. They validate our experience and help us feel understood for a little while, but fail to tell us anything we hadn't considered or tried, or to draw anything out of us which would help us through our difficulties. As an illustration of this we have only to look at the literature on bullying in the workplace. While most of it makes an important contribution and is better than nothing, little of it talks about how to acquire the skills needed to stop the bullying. Most often the steps recommended are along the lines of 'see your union rep' or 'start a grievance procedure'. This is safe advice, but not necessarily much help on its own for someone who is being bullied. In fact, the very act of complaining can escalate the problem!

So I have been studying people who don't have problems. Why do others tend to leave them alone or treat them with respect? What are the skills they use? How did they develop them? And it is the results of my studies that are in this book.

If you meet people who mistreat you, who obstruct you, lie, threaten, manipulate, moan or in any way trouble you or thwart your efforts to lead a more productive life, then this book, I hope, will give you a new slant on how you might approach things differently in future.

Acknowledgements

As is customary at this point I must pay due credit to the people who have helped me in my work. To the many thousands who have attended my seminar series *How to Deal with Difficult People, Creative Relationship Skills,* and *Dealing with Conflict,* particularly those who have shared their experiences with me both before and after using the strategies I suggested. To my clients over the years who have allowed me to see, in a much more intimate way, how doing something different can make a positive change to their lives. And to all my friends, family and colleagues who have helped me in the most testing arena of all – our personal relationships.

Over the years I have read with envy the introductions to many fascinating books where the authors apparently benefited from a small army of researchers, editors, readers and advisors. 'If only...', I would say to myself, bemoaning the fact that I was not in such a fortunate position. Well, things have at last begun to look up and I did get practical help in writing this book. My sincere and respectful thanks to Bernie Sheehan who spent valuable hours reading and editing the first drafts and to Andy Bradbury for his suggestions and proofreading skills, and finally to Madeline Weston who added the index. And special thanks go to my wife, Michelle, who probably knows much more about handling a difficult person than she lets on.

The case studies and examples given in this book are drawn from a wide range of situations. Some are factual and some are composites. In all cases they are sufficiently well disguised to be unrecognisable to the original participants. In particular, I am indebted to the people who, over the years, have kept in touch with me and let me know of their 'stories' as they unfolded. I cannot name them, they know who they are and I offer my sincere thanks for their trust and the confidence they have shown in sharing their journeys with me. Most have now resolved extremely difficult relationships in their lives, all would say they have grown immeasurably as a result and I take my hat off to them for the courage, determination and ingenuity they have shown.

I hope that all these experiences are put together in such a way that you too, on reading this book, will some day say, 'I once had a problem...'

Seaford, East Sussex, 2002

Some terminology

This is a book on how to deal with difficult people and because of comments I have received in the past, I think it would be a good idea to include a few lines on the terminology I have used. It is not my intention to label, brand or judge any individual or group. It has often been pointed out to me that there is really no such thing as a difficult person, only people who use difficult behaviour. Labelling people in this way, critics of the term have said, is unfair and should not be allowed. It is judgemental, simplistic and a label that denies the rich complexity of human nature and the freedom of each to express themselves as their nature dictates. More appropriately, so the party line goes, I should use the term 'difficult behaviour' (as in 'normal person using difficult behaviour'). After all, we can all be difficult sometimes, can't we?

Quite right, and the logical and reasonable part of my nature accepts this. Also, as I shall point out later in the book, when we consider we are being unfairly treated, we will be much more effective if we can remember that it is the behaviour we want to change, rather than the person.

For the sake of simplicity, however, I have adopted the convention of referring to 'difficult people'. I hope that you can indulge me in this and that it will not detract from the usefulness of the book. It is not my intention to label, denigrate or similarly write off any individuals or groups in adopting this approach, but simply to make the reading easier. It is worth adding, too, that if you are one of those unfortunate people who has had to tolerate the difficult behaviour of someone who has consistently manipulated, threatened, intimidated, undermined or in any way denied you the privileges the critics would afford them, then you probably find it very hard to relinquish the term 'difficult person' when thinking of them.

Expediency, too, dictates the use of several adjectives that could be deemed judgemental. Where I have used terms such as 'bad', 'inappropriate', 'wrong' etc, I have intended them as relative and descriptive and not as value judgements.

I have also followed the common editorial practice of using both masculine and feminine pronouns, as well as the informal 'they', throughout the book. This is for the sake of balance and to appease those who might otherwise feel left out. It is not intended to attribute any particular stereotypes or characteristics to either gender. Where I do mention gender psychology I do so clearly and refer to the appropriate literature and research to support my views.

In the same way, I use the term 'marriage' to describe a committed, intimate relationship between two people. I recognise that such unions take various forms and that many committed couples have chosen not to go through a formal ceremony. I make no assumptions regarding gender, the 'marital research' from which I draw my information refers to both heterosexual and same-sex couples.

SECTION 1

Chapter 1
Who are these difficult people?

This book is for anyone involved with others – at work or at home – who wants to achieve more fruitful outcomes in a whole range of relationships. It will help you successfully settle those difficult interactions that just won't resolve themselves.

You can learn to handle apparently impossible situations where people just won't co-operate: ranting bosses, ineffectual co-workers, over-demanding customers, rude or aggressive patients or members of the public who act in unpredictable ways. And it isn't limited to the workplace. If you ever find yourself struggling in your personal relationships there is help here too. This book tells you how to identify different types of difficult people, recognise clues to the patterns in their behaviour, and most importantly – what to do about them.

You will also be given the opportunity to understand how to prepare yourself, so that you become more effective more often in your relationships.

You know those situations where somebody else always seems to get the upper hand? Perhaps they intimidate you or brush aside your well-prepared remarks. It may be they simply seem so superior and arrogant that you are sure they know much more than you, so you don't speak up. Or you may have to deal with one of the silent types, people who just don't react when you are trying to get agreement from them on important issues.

At work our energy and enthusiasm are sapped by people who persistently use difficult behaviour. I have regularly seen entire projects jeopardised because of the behaviour of one person. I have met staff who have changed jobs because they felt unable to improve a relationship with one colleague and I have known many effective and competent managers who have found themselves powerless in the face of the disruptive actions of one or two employees. On the home front we all know of marriages ending in divorce because someone's 'difficult behaviour' was beyond the pale. It is now common to hear of children who demand rather than ask and parents giving in to them because they think it is the easiest course, and schools where there are problems with the attitude of pupils, staff or parents.

Perhaps you have to deal with more than one difficult person. Those of us who work with the public regularly have to face overbearing, demanding, sarcastic or generally rude individuals. Receptionists and call centre staff, for example, are involved in interactions lasting just a few minutes, but they may be subjected to a constant stream of damaging abuse.

Difficult people can be a serious health hazard to individuals and to organisations. They can undermine our best efforts and ruin the quality of our lives. These types of people also cause untold stress in organisations. It is estimated that, in any given situation, there is about a 10 per cent chance of coming up against a difficult person. This means that if you are dealing with the public, every tenth person you meet could become difficult, quite apart from the people you have to deal with inside the organisation such as your boss, co-workers and colleagues. If you work in the public sector, at a telephone call centre or in the complaints department of any sizeable organisation, the chances are that the rate is far higher. As one overstretched and stressed-out doctor's receptionist told me, 'Some days I'm lucky if one in ten of the people I have to deal with are *not* difficult!'

This makes for increasing tension and lost productivity in the workplace, costing employers millions of pounds. It results in stress and misery for employees and a poorer service for customers and service users. And it doesn't stop there. Workers bring that stress home with them, perhaps taking it out on their nearest and dearest; drinking too much, sleeping badly or suffering from other stress-related symptoms, such as headaches, fatigue, lack of motivation or worse.

The reverse happens too. How many people have you known where a stressful personal relationship interfered with their work? This is not to say that we should not be supportive when someone we work with suffers some tragedy or personal difficulty. There are limits, though, to what is acceptable and fitting in the workplace setting. If a personal problem intrudes to a point where it disrupts the work routine on a regular basis, something needs to be done. Since there is a well-proven link between poor relationships, ill-health and an increased likelihood of emotional disturbance such as depression, it could be that someone who is not working as well as they could or who is, for example, constantly demanding attention, actually needs professional help.

The behaviour, not the person

It is important at this stage to illustrate just what I am talking about when I use the term 'difficult people'. When we launched our first series of seminars entitled 'How to Deal with Difficult People' some years ago, a well-meaning manager rang our office to complain (having first let us know that she wasn't being difficult). She pointed out that 'there is no such thing as a difficult person', and went on to say that she had 'disallowed her staff to attend'. Any organisation, she explained, that identified people in this way was in error, since anyone who knew anything about the subject understood that we should be talking about difficult *behaviour,* rather than identifying people as though they are somehow faulty.

And of course, she was quite right.

Nevertheless, faced with difficult behaviour most of us have trouble adopting this generous view, so I use the terms 'difficult people' and 'difficult behaviour' interchangeably. There is a fuller explanation in the terminology section (see page vii).

It also has to be said that we are all somebody's difficult person, sometimes. We can all use obstinacy, moodiness, shouting, criticism, avoidance or any one of dozens of other behaviours from time to time to protect our interests, get our own way or because we are in a bad mood.

If we can keep this in mind it can help to counter the natural tendency many of us have of judging others too quickly. It also makes it easier for us to see things from the other person's point of view; it facilitates how we communicate with them. This is not to say we have to agree with them or accept what they say, but as any competent negotiator knows, it is important to respect a person's right to hold their views (which are, after all, important to them). Frequently, we tend towards finding fault as though making the other person wrong will strengthen our own position. This is the easier option as it requires no great intellectual effort. As one writer on the subject, Robert Bolton, says, 'It is easy to criticise ideas even of an intellectual giant as long as one never addresses the complex problems (they) are trying to understand.'[1] If we can control our natural tendency to criticise we will remain more in control of the situation. This is particularly true where our patience and compassion are being tested to their limits.

The difficult people I am talking about here are the people who are persistently awkward, intimidating, demanding, obstreperous or in any other way constantly disagreeable to a point where they manage to stop us getting on with things the way we would like or the way our job demands. Frequently this comes under the heading of what I would call 'unacceptable behaviour'. There is a line between what is acceptable and what is not that some people just don't respect. It does not matter whether this is deliberate (they have found it works for them so they use it) or incidental (a result of their emotional state or poor social skills). Once the behaviour is persistent and troublesome it entails risks to other staff, the organisation and even the service users.

But the situation may not be so clear-cut. People need not be overtly 'difficult' to cause trouble. You may have to deal with someone who always agrees with you, for example, or who seems to be completely on your side, but who then fails to deliver. Equally, some people use low-key tactics like spreading tittle-tattle or making snide remarks to undermine colleagues. Whatever the approach they use and the context in which it occurs, difficult people behave in such a way that they start to dominate our thoughts and affect the way we think and act. In extreme cases (and I have known plenty) they can make our lives a misery.

Defining difficult people

So, I am referring here to the types of people who persistently use unacceptable behaviour to get their way. I will leave aside for now the complicated issue of judging what is 'unacceptable', because obviously the limits to what each of us considers 'acceptable' behaviour will vary according to personal viewpoint and circumstance. Many social workers, for example, have told me that they will tolerate a certain amount of swearing from a client, but that when the same words are used by their manager (it happens, apparently) they find it unacceptable.

It is in the nature of being human to behave in ways that can irritate others, obstruct progress, get ourselves noticed for the wrong reasons and even end relationships. It is precisely the richness of our range of responses that makes human beings so interesting and adaptable, and it is only to be expected that something as complex and complicated as human interaction would produce as many disasters as it does delights. And for the most part we accept this.

Sometimes, though, we are far too accepting of the negative side of the equation. This may be because we fear reprisals, especially when the offender is someone above us in the hierarchy. But it may also be because we just slide into accepting something we don't like out of politeness or complacency. Many of us can identify a time when we have done this. At first 'it didn't seem worth bothering about' or we 'wanted to avoid a confrontation', only to find that the longer we put up with it, the more we suffer!

And so it is that we regularly tolerate difficult behaviour. We are generally able to put up with demeaning, disrespectful or destructive habits in others for a short time, but when that behaviour becomes persistent, our coping skills start to fail us. Yet so often, rather than sort it out with the difficult person, we put up with it.

Dealing with a dead weight

Frequently, during my seminars and workshops, I have met people who will complain loud and long about the conduct of a colleague, friend or family member. Generally this brings supportive remarks and suggestions from the rest of the group. Paradoxically the complainant will often then respond by playing down their gripes with remarks like 'it's really not that important' or 'they probably didn't mean it'. They continually make excuses for the other person. While tolerance and understanding are qualities to be proud of, they can backfire when we allow ourselves to become a doormat. Often, we'll make all sorts of excuses rather than tackle behaviour we don't like. This is when the trouble starts. Pretty soon, the situation has grown to a point where we find ourselves dealing with the dead weight of a difficult person.

In real life

Natasha was explaining to the group just how difficult it was to work with her long-time colleague Anne. 'The problem is,' she explained, 'everyone in the organisation has rejected her, I seem to be the only friend she has left. It is not that I like working with her, in fact I hate it. She ties up so much of my time with her problems, I can't get on with my work. And she seems less and less able to do hers. I just feel sorry for her and haven't the heart to reject her like everyone else has.'

Natasha told her story during a workshop on Relationships at Work. Suddenly, the facilitator, Jacques Salomé, steps up to her and places his right foot just above her left.

'Tell me,' he asks, 'how would you react if I constantly trod on your toes?'

'Why, I'd move of course!'

'How would you do that?'

Natalie steps back. 'Like this.'

'Exactly, but suppose I followed you, in fact, how about if I hung on to you like this?' Salomé steps up to Natasha, puts both arms around her neck, then he lets his legs collapse under him. Natasha struggles to hold his weight with the man draped around her shoulders. She starts to giggle.

'You OK about that?' he asks.

Natasha is not.

'Why don't you drop me then?'

Natasha, now laughing, replies, 'You might hurt yourself.'

'And you, is this hurting you?'

'Of course, get off please.'

'Oh but I can't, you see I have all these problems. I need someone to lean on.'

Natasha, now visibly niggled, still struggling against the weight of the trainer, says, 'Jacques, please.'

Salomé stands up and places a reassuring hand on Natasha's shoulder.

'You see, if I tread on your toes, you know exactly where your threshold of tolerance is. But with your colleague

Anne, things aren't so clear, are they?'
'From now on they will be,' replies Natasha.

Natasha's example illustrates how supportiveness and forbearance can be misplaced. Her colleague Anne is constantly demanding her time to talk about her problems or tying up Natasha's energies in some way. Natasha naturally wants to be supportive of Anne, and probably started out believing that if she devoted a little time to her, listening and supporting her, it would help Anne in an 'hour of need'. The trouble is that the 'hour' can turn into several months or even years. Anne just does not seem to be operating according to the same set of values as Natasha. Her behaviour is almost certainly not a deliberate strategy to get sympathy, it has become part of her repertoire of coping skills which she has learned to trot out whenever she feels in need. It is even possible that she has been using it for so long she knows no other way of having a conversation. Whatever the cause, Natasha's beliefs about helping and supporting a colleague are conflicting with her professionalism and her wish to be allowed to get on with her job unhindered. Her kindness, far from helping Anne, is unwittingly encouraging her behaviour and may even be preventing Anne from moving on in her own life by developing different ways of responding to her difficulties.

People can impose on our good nature in other ways. For example, you may have had to put up with someone who shouts at you. They act as though they have never learned that a conversation can be a balanced, two-way exchange of views. Every time you raise a topic they respond by raising their voice in a way that stops you in your tracks. Of course, you know you could fight back, but why bother? Anything for a quiet life.

Leaving the handbrake on

I liken taxing or unreasonable behaviour among colleagues to 'driving round town with the handbrake on'. What I mean by this is that many people are enthusiastic about their jobs and come in to work in the morning with the intention of doing a good day's work. This is particularly true in the public sector where I spend so much of my time. Staff here are frequently motivated by a sense of altruism or a wish to help others. It is a source of constant frustration to them when, before getting out to deal with their client group or patients, they have to unravel or in some other way deal with the difficult behaviour of a colleague. Instead of being able to direct all their energies where they are most needed - ie to their clients or service users - they find that they are 'driving round town with the handbrake on'.

If you've ever tried this, deliberately or by accident, you will know that a vehicle with the handbrake on doesn't move along too well; a lot of energy gets burnt up in the back wheels and both the vehicle and the engine suffer. Eventually the damage caused will make expensive maintenance necessary and possibly some parts will have to be replaced. One can easily see the parallels in organisations.

When staff have their valuable energy taken up with repeated interpersonal clashes - quite apart from the cost in time and effort - it raises levels of frustration and reduces motivation and morale. UK organisations waste hundreds of millions of pounds each year in lost productivity, avoidable absenteeism and staff turnover. A large part of this is down to emotional and personal problems arising from behaviour in the workplace.

Estimates of the costs vary, but all agree that they are astronomic. A conservative estimate published in the *Sunday Times* in 2001[2] put the figure at £10.7 billion, but research carried out by the Industrial Society sets the figure a lot higher. 'Stress and low morale are the hidden costs of the UK's £13 billion absenteeism bill' was the headline to its February 2000 press release.[3] To put this in perspective, we are losing the equivalent of 25 per cent of the annual budget for the NHS in England or twice its annual bill for prescriptions.

Relationship maintenance

People value the quality of their relationships at work and all relationships need maintenance. Most species, including our own, spend a substantial part of their time doing just that. The primates most closely related to us can happily while away up to 20 per cent of their day grooming each other. Though this may appear to be an idle pastime with no real purpose, it is in fact a way of building and maintaining alliances and bonds on which the quality of their life in the group depends (quite literally a case of 'you scratch my back and I'll scratch yours').[4] Human beings are also a group species and while we no longer go to the extreme of picking lice off each other for extended periods (though until 300 years ago this was still a cosy practice on long winter evenings in some rural areas of Europe),[5] we symbolically groom each other in other ways. At least, we do if we are wise.

For a species to have survived and evolved to the point where we now dominate the planet, we humans had to develop an incredible range of skills for sizing people up, and for forming and above all maintaining relationships with them. Grooming was one of the practices we used - just like our primate cousins today - to keep our alliances going. Robin Dunbar, professor of psychology at the University of Liverpool, postulates that we developed language as a way of establishing and servicing our relationships. 'Could it be,' he asks, 'that language evolved as a kind of vocal grooming to allow us to bond with ever larger groups than was possible using the conventional primate mechanism of physical grooming?'

So, small talk has a purpose. Those 'watercooler chats' and other brief exchanges we have with our colleagues are actually an essential ritual aimed at preserving social harmony and effectiveness. Gossip is actually of tremendous importance[6] and a little time spent each day talking to those around us about nothing in particular might go a long way.

Unfortunately, the modern workplace leaves little time for such seemingly unproductive pastimes as talking to each other; and where they do, the culture of the organisation often expects measurable outcomes for its indulgence. For example, organised away-days and team-building efforts are intended to 'improve team functioning' or 'bond the workforce'. Increased workloads and a more hectic pace of life at work often mean that our professional relationships suffer. We may only begin to notice the effect of a colleague's difficult behaviour after we have been putting up with it for some time, perhaps because, like Natasha, we will have been making excuses for the other person. Maybe we did not want to make a fuss or simply did not know how to correct what was becoming a problem for us.

Inclusion gives us a social value so our initial reaction when faced with difficult behaviour is to put up with it or excuse it to avoid rocking the boat. This is specially the case with relationships at work where regular contact with our colleagues is obligatory. Speaking up about behaviour we find difficult brings with it the threat of exclusion, reprisal and the risk of being judged 'difficult' ourselves.

Shared values

Frequently there is an added complication. When the difficult behaviour of one individual starts to impact on another, it helps to have some shared values and a common understanding of the ground rules. These can then act as a starting point for discussions aimed at correcting the problem. In short, if there are no boundaries we cannot criticise others for failing to observe them. In many working environments people are thrown together in 'teams', departments are restructured or merged, and staff members come and go. Changes happen and nobody takes the time to stop and think about how the team members are supposed to work together, what they are intending to achieve and more pertinently, what constitutes 'good' behaviour and 'bad'. Such issues are too rarely discussed and the absence of clear guidelines leaves the system open to exploitation and abuse. Even though many of the infractions will be relatively minor and open to interpretation to start with - a colleague refusing to take her share of answering the phone, for example, or another's unexplained absences at critical moments - they can build to become a thorn in the side of colleagues.

Unchallenged, such infractions lead to resentment and a ripple-effect which will spread discontent. Nothing is said but before long feelings are running high and morale is on its way down. Many of the more entrenched cases of difficult behaviour I have come across have been allowed to get that way because the culture of the organisation encouraged it by default. The errant behaviour was never 'nipped in the bud' and the offender may even have been unaware of the trouble they were causing.

Assumptions that any group of individuals will automatically adopt uniform behaviour because they share a set of common values need to be checked, otherwise they can be ingredients in a recipe for failure.

Work suffers, health suffers

Some years ago, I conducted a survey during one of my seminar series. The aim was to find out why people changed their jobs, and what was revealed was surprising.

Over 90 per cent of the respondents who had changed their jobs within the last two years had done so for reasons relating to the quality of relationships in the working environment. In some cases it was undoubtedly that people had been bullied, harassed or intimidated. In others it was simply that they had felt unrecognised or that they had not got from their employers or colleagues the sense of support or recognition they felt they needed or deserved.

A MORI survey of 6,000 nurses published by *Nursing Times* in March 2001 showed that difficult behaviour by colleagues was rife, with one in six of the respondents saying that they had been bullied. The majority were not satisfied with the way the matter was handled by their employer but only half of them had reported the behaviour or made a formal complaint. The report added that over 85 per cent of the nurses who had left their posts because of harassment were dissatisfied with the reaction of their employer.

In a separate study[7] reporting on why nurses quit their profession, a staggering 65 per cent said they would like to leave. One third (22 per cent of sample) said they actually had plans to go and the remaining two thirds (43 per cent) said they would leave if they could think of an alternative career.

Absenteeism

When people are having a difficult time at work many of them will simply change jobs. This is a problem in itself but at least it is visible. Far more worrying are the statistics such as those above that show that many dissatisfied staff don't leave; they stay where they are and their dissatisfaction is expressed in other ways – by taking time off, for example.

The annual average for time off is about eight days per person, with the top scorers in the care sector taking off the equivalent of one month a year in sick leave (19.2 days)[8]. In some of the more stressful working cultures it is seen as a right by staff to take a certain amount of time off in addition to their holiday entitlement. It is common for people to 'take a couple of days off' to deal with the stress caused by someone's difficult behaviour; the more costly effects are long-term sickness and even early retirement under the heading of stress. I spend a great deal of time as a consultant working to persuade organisations of the importance of creating a healthy environment where staff can enjoy more productive relationships.

There have been significant moves in the last 20 years to try and improve things through legislation: anti-harassment policies, anti-bullying campaigns, whistle-blowing legislation and more recently the government's initiatives under the heading of Fairness at Work. Unfortunately, we cannot legislate to make people behave well towards each other. The legislation provides sanctions and indicates a course of action where things have gone wrong. It is less successful in persuading people to work together harmoniously.

Without doubt, a few bad apples can sour the work experience for a large number of people. The effect they can have on the organisation is quite disproportionate to their numbers.[9] This brings me back to my original point: the way that the topic of 'difficult people' is dealt with by so many writers misrepresents the seriousness of the problem. Difficult behaviour in organisations causes havoc. It's costing a huge amount of money in staff turnover, lost productivity, low morale, stress-related problems and it even affects the physical health of staff.

Shared responsibility

I do not wish to lay all the responsibility at the door of employers. We all know of people who fall into the difficult category and they must be held responsible for their own behaviour. Many of them persist despite explicit codes of conduct forbidding offensive or obstructive behaviour. But employers can help by more rigorously demonstrating that interpersonal conflict is unacceptable when it impacts on staff welfare.

It is insufficient to say that a particular person's management style is 'only for the robust'; that members of staff will just have to 'toughen up and deal with the problem of a difficult person' or that 'a certain amount of abuse goes with the territory'. These are all comments that I hear repeatedly.

In real life

Lois was delighted when she got her promotion only six months after joining the company. With so much information to take in, an increased workload and new responsibilities, she knew that her new role would be challenging. What she hadn't bargained for was her manager. He had seemed so agreeable at the interview, but turned out to have a darker side to his nature. Less than a week into her new duties he stormed into her office demanding all sorts of explanations and answers. 'It was crazy, he was apoplectic, firing questions at me that seemed unconnected to the project I was working on.'

And this was not an isolated incident. Before long Lois came to expect at least one of his tirades a week, sometimes they happened more often. Each time the pattern was the same; with no warning the manager would arrive in person or call her, demanding answers to questions she was unprepared to answer. 'It was as though someone had been having a go at him and he just wanted to get his own back,' Lois concluded. 'I tried not to take it personally, but by the end of three months I was on the verge of a breakdown.'

After taking a long weekend to think her situation through, Lois made an appointment to see the director responsible for her department – her manager's manager. 'I knew that the behaviour I was putting up with was wrong,' she said, 'but I thought he was probably under pressure so before I tackled him directly I wanted his boss to be aware of the difficulties I was having. I had expected a bit of support and perhaps an explanation. I also needed to know how to deal with it professionally.'

Lois was not only disappointed, she began to feel utterly hopeless.

'The director told me that I would have to accept my manager's "little idiosyncrasies". What was more sinister, though, was that he told me to toughen up if I wanted to stay in the job. I took this as a veiled threat that I would lose my job if I complained again.'

Lois handed her notice in a few weeks later.

Bad behaviour is something that many working environments tolerate or unwittingly encourage. In certain situations even the most gifted among us can find ourselves having to confront behaviour that exceeds our interpersonal abilities. Lois recognised this and took a first step in the right direction, but quickly saw that she wasn't going to get the help she wanted. She reasoned that the problem was endemic in the department, and although she loved her job, she decided that she would be unable to change the situation and was not prepared to work under such circumstances.

While I would not wish to exaggerate the situation – and I recognise that claims of unjust treatment have sometimes been unfairly exploited by staff – this remains an essential problem in organisations today. Many of them foster a climate where difficult behaviour can proliferate, and they fail to take adequate steps to correct it. In the words of the '70s cult TV programme *The Six Million Dollar Man*: 'We have the technology'. We can make our workplaces happier, more productive and healthier places if only we can generate the vision and long-term commitment.

Pool of resources

In our personal relationships we can benefit from a huge pool of information about how to keep our relationships healthy and in good working order. First there is the cultural wisdom present in every society, which, though a little out of fashion in the modern westernised world, is nonetheless sound. Qualities such as tolerance, compassion, patience or the ability to reflect on our own behaviour may now be viewed more as a means to an end (to be used in order to *get* something) rather than an end in themselves (to be used in order to *be* something), but many of those things our grannies taught us have lasted through hundreds of generations because they are of value. 'Always do unto others...' or 'Never let the sun go down on your wrath' are not only commonsense injunctions, they can also be used as handy directives for living.

Another source of advice on how to handle our personal interactions is a wide-ranging body of serious psychological research. Many authors have given us the means of understanding more about how we handle ourselves in our relationships (see bibliography). Much of the research has been directed at specific target groups, for example, couples or families, but the essential skills remain the same for all human relationships.

This pool of information tells us not only that personal relationships require regular maintenance, but also how to do it.

It would, of course, be unreasonable to expect individuals or employers to totally eradicate difficult behaviour, but more could take serious steps to discourage it and combat the pernicious side effects.

Choose your strategy

Most people handle the difficult people in their lives pretty well most of the time. Occasionally we come up against behaviour that exceeds our normal abilities and it is for those situations that I have written this book. It will also be useful if you simply want to know more about how human interactions can be influenced towards successful outcomes.

I do not wish to suggest that we are surrounded by difficult people, because we are not. But we are living in increasingly pressured times and I believe that social trends are making life more stressful, not less. This is exacerbated by the fact that the traditional social binders are falling out of fashion and putting us at increased risk - in public at least - of rude or inconsiderate behaviour. Politeness and respect for others are now so rare in some quarters that we can be surprised when they occur and even suspect the motive. Our society is paying scant attention to ensuring that future generations are able to get along better than we do at the moment.

It is not all bad. I know from the experiences of hundreds of individuals I have spoken to in recent years just how resourceful people can be. But I also know that every time I have met someone who is enjoying successful and supportive relationships that this success was not an accident. They worked at it.

Nor am I suggesting that reading a book or even dozens of books will make you a better person or a more successful one. Taking the time to read up on the subject and think about it, however, can be invaluable in improving how we interact with others. Since the only part of the equation we can be sure of having any impact on is our own behaviour, this is a good place to start.

Rules and regulations laid down by governments, employers and others are useful in telling us how they would like us to behave towards each other, but remember that most of these rules will have been put in place as controls - in other words, in response to bad behaviour that is already happening. Anti-harassment policies and the like come into being precisely because we recognise that some people are likely to harass others. By the time we need to resort to using such policies for our own protection, things have generally gone too far to be improved by other means. I would be interested to hear whether anyone who has had to resort to invoking such a policy has found that it improved their relationship with the person(s) they were complaining about.

At the end of the day we control our own interactions and the ideas I am putting forward here will help. They are drawn from a wide range of sources and have been shown to work, provided that they are used with sincerity and conviction. All of the tactics I mention have evolved with the help of others and I must pay tribute to them for that. In particular I am grateful to the many people who have kept in touch and let me know about their progress with the difficult person in their lives.

Difficult behaviour can and should be addressed and I make suggestions for working round the perpetrators, rather than changing them. I have provided some scripts that make the principles of the interactions clearer, and I have named seven patterns of difficult behaviour with titles such as 'The Steamroller' and 'The Guerrilla' (see Chapter 8) to make identification easier. I know that this is over-simplistic, as any system of labelling categories of behaviour is bound to be. I am not suggesting that we can cram the rich diversity of human behaviour into just seven headings. There must be as many ways to be difficult as there are people on earth. I have chosen these categories as a way of stereotyping certain frequently occurring behaviour patterns that have been observed by myself and others. These headings also provide a handy way of illustrating a large number of strategies for dealing with difficult people.

Many people have immediately identified the type of behaviour relevant to the difficult person in their lives in one of these seven categories. Others have told me that, for them, things were not so cut-and-dried. A woman attending one of my seminars told me, 'My father-in-law uses all of these behaviours'. If the behaviour of the person you want to handle is neatly contained in one of the characters, so much the better. The strategies I suggest will be similarly outlined. If, on the other hand, the person is using a range of difficult tactics you may have to combine parts of several different characters' strategies. I have also provided several bullet-pointed approaches as an aid to self-management in tricky situations.

With a little preparation you can handle the difficult people in your life more productively. There are, however, a couple of provisos:

1. Always know your own cut-off point. Retain the ability to change your mind and 'do something different' if your chosen strategy isn't working. Remember, too, that with some behaviour the best policy really is to ignore it.

2. If your situation is serious - if you are being bullied, harassed or are at risk from physical attack - look after yourself before trying to handle or modify the other person's behaviour. There are some relationships where we lose ground to a point where we start to suffer emotionally. This is not the time to attempt new strategies - it is a time to get help. If the behaviour is happening at work it is illegal and the responsibility of your employer to do something about it.

Difficult behaviour seems to be on the increase and it ranges from petty and disruptive to positively dangerous.

Where it puts people's personal safety at risk it is time for professional advice rather than self-help books. In the next chapter I ask whether our society really is becoming angrier and outline the scale of the challenge we are facing.

Chapter 2
The social context

Other people's difficult behaviour can be a nuisance that preoccupies us. In both our working and personal relationships, situations can arise where we spend a disproportionate amount of time thinking about difficult behaviour, wondering what causes it and planning how to deal with it. We can waste so much time analysing it that by the time we eventually make up our minds about to how to react we actually do nothing. 'Better to let sleeping dogs lie,' we say, or 'It's water under the bridge'. Often, part of the reason for this is that we have trouble in actually identifying what constitutes difficult behaviour. In its most extreme form, of course, such as when someone is visibly angry or when they blatantly disagree with us, it is obvious. Unpleasant though it is, at least we know we don't like it. We can identify it in order to tackle it (though, astonishingly, in the workplace we frequently don't).

A different sort of problem arises when we feel as though something is wrong but can't actually pin it down. We can all think of situations where we have been on the receiving end of behaviour we felt uncomfortable with but which was so subtle or low-key that we were unsure of how to respond: for example, when a colleague is always just a little bit late, or that they promise one thing and then do another. People can also act in a way that sends out mixed messages; for example, they may make 'good natured' jibes at our expense. These negative comments masquerading as jokes can be incredibly difficult to deal with and can have all sorts of nasty consequences if ignored (see Dealing with a Guerrilla on page 135). Another example of confusing signals is when our 'friends' tell us what others think of us or our actions; the only trouble is, they seem to have an overwhelming need to focus on the negative views and never the positive. Worse, they may feel the need to let us in on what others are saying about us... even when we don't ask. Such sniping gossip is never positive or flattering, but more likely a way of criticising us indirectly.

The range of tactics used by difficult people is as wide and varied as people themselves. At one end of the spectrum they are so subtle as to make us doubt our own sanity, the reliability of our memory or our interpretation of events. At the other end the behaviour is highly visible and openly hostile. Incidents involving belligerent or aggressive behaviour are for many people a daily occurrence, so let's look at something that seems to be becoming emblematic of society today: anger.

Are we getting more angry?

One of our modern media givens is that people are getting angrier. We take it as read that we are becoming increasingly intolerant, short-tempered and discourteous towards each other. Radio, television and newspaper reports regularly launch into descriptions of angry or violent incidents that generally support the assumption that levels of anger and violence have increased dramatically in recent years. We have even started to build a terminology around it. 'Air rage' was first reported in 1988, incidents of road rage are so frequent they don't even make the news any more and the number of other rages is growing daily: queue rage, lift rage, 'phone rage, restaurant rage, gym rage... the list goes on.

Anger is on everyone's lips. In one incident I witnessed recently a woman in her twenties let rip a stream of foul invective at someone in a car park she suspected of blocking her in. When the victim explained that he was not the owner of the offending car she eventually realised her mistake and apologised – for her bad language – but justified it with 'Sorry, but I was angry, all right?' Another example is the male employee with almost 30 years' experience as a surveyor, driven to the brink by the behaviour of his – much younger – manager and another colleague. He described to me how 'they both used to shout and swear at me on a daily basis. Eventually I cracked.' He was on long-term sick leave 'for stress' when he told me this.

In the first case being angry was apparently sufficient reason for the woman to verbally abuse a complete stranger (and in the process put herself at risk since she had no way of knowing how he might respond). The surveyor's story is more tragic but it implicitly makes the same point; I am sure the other two people involved would justify their behaviour in some way. Perhaps it is cases like these that have encouraged magistrates to add anger management courses to the list of penalties they can impose for anti-social behaviour. Such initiatives are not limited to adults. In July 2001 Estelle Morris – then Minister of Education – defended moves to introduce anger management classes for five and six year olds.

Apparently society is getting angrier and as a result a whole anger industry has grown up. A quick search on the internet using the term 'anger management' yielded 59,100 sites (and that is just in the English language) and the phrase 'difficult people' scored 38,000. Contrast this with two topics that are supposed to be major preoccupations in peoples' lives: sex, with 50,000 addresses, generated almost 20 per cent less than anger (sex is also an international term and so the search was not restricted to the English language), and 'money' brought in a mere 31,200 sites. Anger tops the ratings.

Escalator rage

George hurried along the platform intent on making it to the mainline station to catch the 16.44 train for home. As the crowd jockeyed for positions to step on to the escalator he hesitated a moment to let a young couple struggling with three bags between them pass in front of him. As they positioned themselves with their luggage to stand on the right of the moving staircase he quickly slid through to their left. He had been intending to keep moving up the escalator but as he started a loud voice stopped him. 'Oi, a bit of patience wouldn't be a bad thing!' George turned. The young man, who was sweating under the weight of a large rucksack slung round his chest, glowered at him; his girlfriend, head down, said nothing. 'Yeah, I meant you.' George – 50 years old and a trained negotiator – was no stranger to hostility. He took one look at the offender and, recognising the futility of a discussion, decided the best course of action was simply to end the conversation as quickly and non-confrontationally as possible. 'I'm sorry, I didn't mean to…' The first speaker cut him off, hostility rising. 'Your sort piss me off.' He cocked his head back defiantly. George just responded with 'I apologised, let's just leave it there.'

'I couldn't believe it,' George told me later, 'there we were, both on a crowded, moving escalator and this guy was spoiling for a fight. If anything had happened there could have been a very nasty accident. He was acting like a bullying yob. I just wanted to get my train.'

The tormenter stepped up his verbal assault, adding mimicry of George's middle-class accent to his other insults. 'Oh! Let's just leave it there,' he aped. George had one last try. 'You accused me of impatience, I have apologised, let's keep it courteous.'

'It was not me who caused the trouble in the first place, Mister-bloody-smart-arse in your poncey shirt and tie.'

'OK, that'll do, I'm going.'

'Yeah, piss off, piss off before I get the hump with you,' hissed the youth.

George made his train, and though angry he soon calmed down and reviewed the situation. 'I think the only ending he wanted was to have a fight. I had a crack at calming things down, but in the end the only thing to do was to

ignore the insults and walk away. I was happy to be able to,'
was George's summary.

It seems that everyone has a similar story or knows
someone who has. People are pressured, courtesy is lacking,
incivility reigns and the social controls which have enabled
humans to develop, live and work together are disintegrating.
In the words of Spencer Carter, professor of law at Yale
University, 'We are now far more likely to grow angry... and
snap at the next person we see.' [1]

The thin end of the wedge

What stories like George's illustrate is that standards of
behaviour in public are falling, and that however well intended
and socially compliant our own behaviour, we cannot
guarantee the conduct of others. Fortunately most people are
civil most of the time, but the trends are moving in the wrong
direction and in the words of Professor Carter again, 'incivility
is a force multiplier and the forces it multiplies are negative.'
Bad behaviour breeds bad behaviour. Unless we make a
conscious effort to control the way we act and respond to
others we will all suffer from this decline.

So the question of whether we are getting angrier is easily
answered with an intuitive 'yes'. It is not so easily answered
scientifically because there is very little research into people's
behaviour at what I'd call the 'low end' of the scale. That is,
rudeness, discourtesy and arguments that do not end in
violence or overt threat. Studies are constantly being published
on violence and aggression, crime rates, divorce, bullying and
harassment, but very little is known – in terms that can be
quantified and monitored – about our millions of daily
interactions and how we experience them. That things seem to
be getting worse is based on impressions rather than hard facts.

Reports of attacks involving violence have increased in sectors like nursing, transport and social work, and since almost all such assaults are preceded by verbal abuse we can safely assume that levels of verbal abuse have risen too.

Figures from the British Crime Survey 2000 show that while there was a small overall increase in violent incidents at work from 1997 to 1999, the patterns of threats and assaults were different; assaults increased by 21 per cent while threats actually fell by 7 per cent. Separating 'assaults' from 'threats' in this way can be misleading; 'threat' in this context means verbal abuse that did not result in violence, whereas 'assault' presumably does not exclude the almost inevitable verbal warnings that are known to precede violence in most cases.[2] The results of the survey therefore seem to support the contention that the public expression of anger is increasing even though the report summary attempts to minimise the increase with the words, 'However, neither change was statistically significant.'

Few people would deny that the evidence of difficult and abusive behaviour is all around us. But much of this is of the 'not like it was in my day' or the 'things have changed since I did my training' variety. When it comes to plotting measurable trends we have nothing to go on as a starting point. Professional bodies like Unison, the TUC, the Royal College of Nursing, teachers' unions, the Medical Defence Union and others have told me that they are aware of the problems of difficult behaviour that their members face and some even say they have carried out surveys. Quantifiable evidence, however, is very hard to come by. One exception to this is the study carried out by Dr Sean Neill at Warwick University for the National Union of Teachers (NUT). He found that four out of five teachers believed that they have seen a deterioration in their pupils' behaviour since joining the profession and 60 per cent said that it was 'very much worse'. There is a consensus that these days many more children are coming into the school system who lack the basic social skills of handling their own emotions, particularly anger. In a recent article on the subject, one teacher's remarks illustrate an increasingly common experience for many: 'Members of staff are bitten, kicked or pushed by angry or distressed children.'[3]

In my own work – when conducting surveys to establish levels of violence and aggression in organisations – I often get the response that things have got worse 'over the last two years'. There is a consistency to this response that is surprising because, regardless of the professional context or geographical area, the figure that regularly comes up is two years: not one, three or four, always two. Secondly, I have been hearing this for at least ten years. There seems to be a uniformity in the way people report (or remember) the levels of difficult behaviour they are experiencing in their work.

Increased pressure

Since researchers in this area tend to be conservative, it is not clear from studies whether there has actually been an increase in levels of public expressions of anger, or whether the perceived increase is due to less tolerance coupled with greater awareness. Certainly in recent years incidents of verbal abuse and assaults on people in all walks of life have increased. This is particularly noticeable in the public sector, transport and other areas where staff deal with large numbers of the public. In many sectors increased expectations among consumers of the service has led to higher expectations. This has been accompanied by dwindling resources and a gradual reduction in staffing levels. This combination of circumstances quickly becomes a recipe for disaster that is often not handled well by employers. The resulting pressure on staff inevitably means that they come under pressure from two directions: from their clients or customers on the one hand and from pressured colleagues on the other. One of the ironies of today's workplace relations is that staff say they feel beleaguered by the ever-increasing demands placed on them and they take out their frustration on managers by blaming them for lack of acknowledgement and support for the difficulties they face. Survey after survey on attitudes show that many staff see their managers as lacking sensitivity, avoiding important issues or failing to act supportively in times of crisis. Speak to their managers and you will hear the same stories except that they blame the directors! We are all in the same boat but instead of bringing us together this tends to be divisive. The tendency on both sides is to step up the sorts of behaviour we call difficult.

The increasing demand in so many situations to get 'a quart from a pint pot' is placing a huge demand on how people work together. The very things that are so often sacrificed in order to increase productivity and make better use of resources – regular breaks, a canteen, opportunities for staff to meet and discuss things informally – are precisely the things we need to keep ourselves sane and able to cope with the extra demands we are facing. Despite the management rhetoric of the last two decades about the need to make the workplace more people-friendly, the trend in many quarters is to push ever harder for measurable results. Not surprisingly, this will often bring out the worst in people.

There is no doubt that staff in all walks of life are having to deal with an increasingly demanding and strident public, and that this impacts on their health and well-being. Unfortunately, it is not restricted to customers and service users. Colleagues give them grief as well!

Workplace morale

It is hardly surprising that the difficult behaviour of colleagues underlies many staff complaints about low morale at work. It quickly becomes part of a vicious cycle: when people are under pressure, stressed and fed-up it tends to bring out the worst in them, this in turn has the knock-on effect of lowering the spirits of their co-workers and repeating the cycle. The CBI reports that of the 192 million working days lost each year, 80 per cent are attributable to short-term absences[4] While it acknowledges that most absences are genuinely thought to be the result of sickness, the report also cites low morale as a contributory factor to these high rates of short-term absence. Similarly, the Industrial Society says that emotional and personal problems cause a high rate of absence; according to employees' self-certification forms, it is the fifth most common reason for staying away from work. Significantly, managers believe it is actually more common; they place it second in order of importance.

In the more extreme cases that are regularly reported to us, staff have opted for being signed off with long-term stress-related illness because they no longer know how to deal with a difficult person at work.

A survey carried out on behalf of the GMB union found that 49.8 per cent of NHS respondents say they have been harassed or bullied at work. The main source, they said, was their own managers![5] A separate study of 6,000 NHS staff conducted in March 2001 showed a general lack of confidence in the way managers deal with complaints of harassment. The Industrial Society reported in June 2001 that job satisfaction is a better predictor of economic performance in organisations than competitive strategy, market share or the amount of money spent on research and development. The UK, the report said, has the lowest levels of employee satisfaction among the leading European countries. There were many reasons for this dissatisfaction, the Society said, but the report focused on the way staff were managed, communications, and training and development as the main reasons. Roger Elgin, writing in *The Times* on conflict in the office, said, 'One of the most common reasons why people find themselves out of a job is failure to get on with their bosses or disputes with colleagues.'[6]

Job satisfaction is one of those intangible factors that some innovative employers have tried to build into the workplace, though sadly such groundbreaking initiatives are still rare. This is a pity because psychologists have for years been making the link between job satisfaction and those more tangible assets beloved of accountants: staff retention, productivity, customer loyalty and the most powerful argument of all: profit. A leading authority on the psychology of personal fulfilment has commented, 'When there is reason to think that we are appreciated, job satisfaction is usually high; whereas the greatest source of stress in the workplace is the feeling that no one is interested in supporting our goals. Infighting among co-workers, inability to communicate with superiors and subordinates are the bane of most jobs.' [7]

Professor Andrew Oswald of the University of Warwick has prepared an international job satisfaction league table. 'For a prosperous nation, we do a lot less well on the latest job satisfaction rating than we should,' he said. He places the UK at number 17 on his list, behind Denmark, the Philippines, Cyprus, Swizerland and Israel among others. [8]

How health suffers

One of the most worrying aspects of this is that the relationships we count on most – in both our private and working lives – can actually put us at risk. Healthy relationships can act as a refuge from the turmoil and strain of daily life 'out there'. Conversely, there is a direct and proven link between dysfunctional relationships and ill-health. Take, for example, the sad inevitability that half of all sufferers of depression are living in a dysfunctional marriage and that, similarly, in half of all unhappy marriages one of the partners is clinically depressed. [9]

Our physical health suffers too when our relationships are battlegrounds. The break-up of a marriage causes physical as well as mental harm. Stress suppresses the immune system so there is an increased vulnerability to infectious diseases, and there are links between the quality of intimate relationships and other physical ailments. Cancer, chronic pain, cardiac disease, allergies, pulmonary disorders and musculo-skeletal disorders are just some of the complaints that have been shown to have associations.[10] Dr John Gottman, the world-renowned researcher into marital success and failure, says the negative effects of a poor marital relationship also include increased rates of road traffic accidents (including fatalities), suicide, violence, shorter lifespan and increased mortality from disease.[11] Other researchers point to increased alcohol and substance misuse, greater risk of sexually transmitted disease and work-related problems.

Conversely, a good relationship offers protection against health risks. Just as couples with ongoing marital difficulty have a higher risk of psychological and other disorders, so being part of a marriage or other stable, intimate relationship that is rated high in satisfaction has been shown to have a beneficial effect. There is less risk to the partners of psychiatric illness, more resistance to the negative effects of major stressors such as unemployment, and less likelihood of a chronic illness. [12]

Negativity loves failure

There are, of course, many differences between personal relationships and those at work. What is of interest are the common factors which have a specific link to difficult behaviour. Chief among these is the natural human propensity towards negativity or pessimism, and its side-effects such as low morale and even a sense of hopelessness. Positive, upbeat people are easier to work with because they tend to radiate optimism. Negativity, on the other hand, can quickly destroy any optimism and leads to back-biting, complaining and other destructive habits.

That negativity might be expressed as outright hostility, as in the escalator example above, but it may also be far more low-key, like put-downs or failure to engage fully in discussions. In terms of dealing with the behaviour we find difficult, it is very often the ambiguous situations – the neighbours who let the dog bark all night, the colleague who is always late back from lunch, the person who regularly parks across our driveway – that we find most difficult to deal with. As we saw in Chapter 1, we will quite often make excuses for the other person rather than approach them about the habit we find troublesome because we fear the outcome in some way.

If we can genuinely let things go because they don't bother us, or can rationalise our own feelings and accept the things that irk us with good grace, all well and good. It is when we can't do this that we start to make problems for ourselves. If we regularly deny the sense of unfairness or injustice we are feeling at someone else's thoughtless, manipulative or deliberately selfish behaviour – however well we try to hide it – it is not long before our resentment starts to leak out through the veneer we have used to conceal it. This is the point at which we start to become a difficult person ourselves.

In real life

Jane was becoming increasingly grumpy at work. She used to love her job as a waitress in a fashionable country hotel. Then Sarah arrived. She was younger and less experienced than Jane but her sense of humour was popular with the guests, and the tips they left showed it. Jane found her over-familiar but she could not criticise Sarah for that, it was more her youth and vivacity that were against her.

Within two weeks of Sarah taking the job, Jane's behaviour towards her new colleague was becoming difficult. She would deliberately and very obviously check all the tables when Sarah had finished setting them, or she would undermine Sarah when she was serving a table with an intrusive 'Is everything alright?' Even though Sarah clearly had everything in hand when things were busy, on one occasion Jane insisted on taking over some of her tables for her. It was not long before a couple on one of the tables – frustrated by the delay since Jane took over – started to try and catch Sarah's eye. This only irritated Jane all the more and she icily put the customers in their place.

For her part, Sarah was at a loss for what to do. When she had first arrived in the job she had sensed Jane's unease and made allowances for her. 'I didn't want to rock the boat,' she said. Unfortunately the atmosphere between them got increasingly tense and at one point, when Sarah accidentally served soup to a customer who had ordered a different starter, she suspected Jane of having switched the plates laid ready for her in the kitchen.

Jane became openly hostile towards Sarah. Everything she did seemed to annoy Jane, and Jane's demeanour changed. From previously having been an efficient, valued and reliable member of staff she became someone who constantly wore an expression of annoyance and interfered in ways that did not concern her.

Sarah, too, started to change. She would no longer greet customers brightly as they arrived in the restaurant. At times she became sullen and appeared unmotivated.

When Bob the manager began to notice the change in Sarah he was concerned. On a couple of occasions, as they closed up in the evening, he had asked Sarah if everything was all right and she had simply responded 'fine'. When he specifically asked her if she had any difficulties because he had noticed the change in her work (and the tips were down), she became defensive and insisted that there were no problems.

When I met Sarah she had left the restaurant and taken an office job. 'I really loved the restaurant because I like interacting with people and I enjoyed everything about the job. It is just that Jane was making things so difficult

> that I could not stay.' When I asked her why she didn't
> tackle Jane about her behaviour sooner, nip it in the bud,
> so to speak, she replied, 'I didn't want to let on, I thought
> if I ignored the problem it would go away.'

Sarah's initial patience with her colleague is understandable. Arriving in a new job she was uncertain of how to deal with her more experienced co-worker, and as Jane's disagreeable behaviour was at first quite low-key it was also hard for the younger woman to tackle it. She was worried about appearing petty or a troublemaker herself. Before long, though, the barely concealed hostility between the two women was causing a real problem. The difficulty now was the tensions between them; when feelings are running high it is difficult to discuss things without them getting out of hand. Sarah worried that she'd only make things worse. She was a good communicator and, as her relationship with the customers showed, a likeable and approachable person. She would certainly have been able to empathise with Jane and probably avoid problems altogether if she had devoted a little time to the problem early on.

Meaning versus Impact

The spectrum of behaviours that we find difficult is wide and diverse. Some of the more persistent and less ambiguous types of strategies that difficult people resort to have got names which are self-explanatory: bullying, harassment, racial prejudice, stalking and malicious communications, for example. A range of situations where people have suffered as a result of ill-treatment at work have been fairly adequately tested in the courts or through tribunals. Most organisations have codes of conduct or policies for dealing with such extreme cases, even though the processes involved can be as tough on the individuals making the complaints as they are on the perpetrators. Of necessity, since our legal system is an adversarial one, any time we invoke the law to settle a dispute there is going to be a 'winner' and a 'loser'. This can be so unhealthy for individuals and organisations that often extreme difficult behaviour goes unchallenged.

In any event, such instances are largely beyond the scope of this book. But it is worth remembering the typical pattern of unpleasant behaviour. People who have become victims of the extreme behaviour described above have frequently told me that it started out with a bit of idle banter that didn't seem worth challenging. Over time the behaviour escalated to a point where they felt unable to do anything about it and their health and well-being started to suffer. It seems that how we respond early on – particularly with bullying but also with other unfair treatment – determines whether things get worse or whether the perpetrator will leave us alone. ̄

Some forms of difficult behaviour, if left unchallenged, can escalate into something much worse. My advice is, if you find someone's behaviour persistently unacceptable then talk to them about it early on, while it is still possible to do so without too much emotion. That way you are more likely to be objective about it and reduce the risk of them responding defensively because they feel attacked.

When we do tackle people about their behaviour, there is a standard set of responses: they say they were unaware of being difficult or offensive, that it was not their intention to do harm, or that it was just a joke. These are also the sorts of excuses their victims use to avoid tackling the behaviour in the first place.

If we have been offended, the fact that someone declares that their regularly misplaced comments were not intended to hurt or that their jokes at our expense were 'just a bit of fun' does nothing to mitigate their *impact*. And it is the impact of the comments we must do something about, whatever the intention behind them. In fact, as we'll see later, getting into a debate about intentions and interpretations is one of the quickest ways of disempowering ourselves in such cases.

Incivility or insensitivity?

These days we are subjected to such a steady flow of information on relationships, at work or elsewhere, that there are very few valid excuses for anyone to be unaware of the need to monitor their behaviour towards others. Whether it is provoked by anger, stress, impatience or any of the many side-effects of humans under pressure, from the moment we start to live or work among others it is up to each of us to watch the less desirable facets of our behaviour. We all have our blind spots, but there are limits to what it is reasonable and fair to expect those around us to tolerate.

It follows that any time we allow someone else to treat us unfairly to a point where we are beginning to get upset by it, we are not only failing to protect ourselves but also doing them a disservice by unwittingly reinforcing the behaviour. Furthermore, in the words of one wit, 'We are also denying them an opportunity for growth.' After all, the evolution of the human race has been based not just on biological and psychological development, but has to a huge extent depended on our socialisation as a species. The ability to get along in groups is fundamental to our survival and our prosperity in every sense of the word.

I am therefore making the case that it is entirely healthy and proper to continue to educate one another about our needs and expectations, provided that this is done in a dignified and mutually respectful manner. There are certain provisos to this which I shall outline in the next chapter.

Whenever people live or work together there will be difficult behaviour to contend with and to a large extent we tolerate this. When it becomes overt, persistent or destructive the chances are that it threatens someone's well-being and possibly even that of the group. As we have seen, the trends in society seem to indicate a gradual decline in behaviour, and things will not improve unless helped along. In what I have called 'extreme' cases, policies and the law can impose sanctions on the offenders, but such 'top down' approaches will be slow to change peoples' opinions and beliefs. The Sex Discrimination Act, for example, has been in force in the UK since 1975 yet almost 30 years on no one could argue that women and men enjoy equal status in the workplace. In the same vein, we have not seen many genuine improvements in racial equality since the introduction of the Race Relations Act in 1976.

Taking things into our own hands

I am not advocating tackling major social injustices here, I am promoting the idea that it is worthwhile adopting a consistent approach in our dealings with the difficult people in our lives so that they will be 'encouraged' to be more correct in their behaviour towards us. The following chapters include many tried and tested approaches to this.

All too often I have met people who were suffering because of the treatment being meted out to them. On many other occasions people have told me that their lives would improve if only someone else would change. Some difficult person in their lives always seemed to get the upper hand. Well, as Eleanor Roosevelt said, 'No one can make you feel inferior without your consent.' If this has been happening to you, it may be time to respectfully withdraw that consent.

Chapter 3
Guiding principles

Before starting out

Over the years that I have been speaking to people about managing difficult behaviour in others, I have found it useful to outline what I'd call the guiding principles. These are common sense pointers to keeping interactions healthy, respectful and balanced. They will help you to avoid the common pitfalls of dealing with difficult behaviour such as loss of respect, power struggles or embarking on a strategy that will only make matters worse. It is important to consider these points at the outset to reduce the risk of:

Accidentally weakening your own position

The strategies and ideas I have outlined in this book can dramatically improve your results in dealing with tricky situations. Applied properly they will help you to circumvent difficult behaviour and even in some cases re-educate the offender. But there is a warning: any strategy needs a little planning. Fail to prepare sufficiently and you run the risk of simply making things worse. Before implementing the techniques and pointers included in the following chapters, take the time to practise and plan your strategy, otherwise you could undermine your own best efforts.

Attacking or 'point scoring'

Understandably, anyone who has been on the receiving end of difficult behaviour can start to feel a little aggrieved. Before long they risk becoming emotionally involved in the situation and will have difficulty viewing it dispassionately. Once we are 'hooked' in this way we are at a major disadvantage because our reason is likely to be tainted by our need for revenge or, at best, to show the other person the error of their ways. This can lead us into 'point scoring' that will simply escalate any difficult situation. Of course, most of us think of ourselves as reasonable people (especially when we are being unreasonable), and believe we are capable of remaining honest, fair and objective even when aroused. Alas, this is not so. Think of a time when you have been irritated or angry with someone and the way you have doggedly clung to a point which – once you had calmed down – you were ruefully able to see from a wider perspective. When we are emotionally aroused it becomes very difficult to remain objective and honest with ourselves. If your aim is point scoring or 'winning', I suggest you look somewhere else. Join a debating society or take up boxing.

When I explain this to the audience during my seminars I always notice one or two disappointed expressions. It is human nature to want to 'get even' when we feel wronged. It is even enshrined in the popular saying 'Don't get mad, get even'. But I don't think this separation is really possible. If you are thinking of getting even you are, by definition, still mad at the other person.

Misunderstanding what we can and can't do

Has anyone ever tried to change you? How did you react? Did you thank them for pointing out the error of your ways and promise to do better in future? I'll bet you did! The chances are that you promptly responded by digging in your heels. If we are prepared to be influenced at all, it is generally only when the suggestions are made to us in the context of a mutually respectful and supportive relationship. In other words we are generally only prepared to consider changing our habits when the other person's opinion matters to us.

It is extremely unlikely that anyone will willingly change their ways at the request or suggestion of another person when their relationship is marked by tension, pressure or difficult behaviour on either side (if you are already able and willing to do this you probably won't be reading this book). Any strategy which relies on getting the other person to change without having first built a relationship of trust and respect (I'll cover this idea in more detail later) will probably fail. Of course, some people do manage to pressurise, manipulate, intimidate or coerce the other person into submission, and they do not always appear overtly unpleasant, but such arrangements come with a cost because they are based on rules which then have to be enforced. As my Granny used to say, 'Any time you use rules to get someone to do something, you'll have to become a policeman.' [1]

A similar point was made by theologian and political activist Reinhold Niebuhr when he wrote the Serenity prayer in 1943:

God give us grace to accept with serenity
the things that cannot be changed,
courage to change the things which should be changed
and the wisdom to distinguish the one from the other.

This first stanza, the best known and most often quoted part of the poem, eloquently captures the sentiment of the whole; that we will be happiest when we understand that some things (and people) will not be changed just because we would like them to be.

It is important to understand the limits of our influence in a given situation and not to overestimate the control we have. If we respond in kind when others try to control, coerce or manipulate us, we simply perpetuate the problems we are trying to address.

Fighting fire with fire

When our interactions with others are healthy and balanced we are more likely to have positive outcomes. Even when our attempts fail, we are at least able to come out of the encounter emotionally intact and unhindered by regret or recrimination. On the other hand, if we lack a guiding framework there is a greater chance that we will slip into the sort of negative behaviour driven by a need to control or dominate the other person. At this point we start to fight fire with fire and become difficult people ourselves.

The five principles

1. Listen well and with empathy

The catchphrase to remember here is 'First seek to understand'. You have probably noticed that most of us, particularly when we feel we are under pressure, work hard to put our own point of view across first. Indeed, this will very often interrupt or interfere with our ability to really hear what is going on around us. It is essential that we develop our own listening skills and that we demonstrate a listening stance to the other person. One of my mantras is that if only we could learn to listen as a society – and I think we should be teaching listening skills to children in school – then we could reduce our problems across the board by as much as 50 per cent. Listening is the key to all the strategies that I shall be talking about, not only because we will learn to understand better what the other person is saying but also because it is important to listen out for patterns of behaviour. I shall say more about this later.

When we are engaged in any sort of difference of opinion the uppermost thought in our minds is to be heard. We struggle to put our point across at all costs and the result is often what the French call a 'dialogue des sourds' (literally, a conversation between deaf people) [2], when neither person is hearing the other's point of view. But think about this for a moment. If you have ever been in such a situation, what was the most important thing to you when you were trying to make yourself heard? I'm willing to bet that, first and foremost, you wanted a sign that the other person was paying attention. You wanted to know they were listening. In the first instance the most important thing is that we feel that our views can be heard, understanding comes later. Furthermore, we are more likely to escalate our attempts at getting attention than we are to step up our demands to be understood (there is no point in seeking understanding with someone who appears not to be listening). After all, most of us cope better with being misunderstood than we do with being ignored.

Listening is the single most important skill available to us in resolving difficulties and it is the least widely studied in lessons on communication. Not surprisingly, I think that feeling unheard is also at the root of a great many social ills. What happens if someone does not appear to be listening to you? How do you respond? Chances are you step up your efforts to be heard by raising your voice, shouting or some other sort of behaviour designed to get you the attention you think you deserve. In extreme cases of feeling unheard, people will vote with their feet and just not turn up for work for a day or two, leave a relationship, or use some other behaviour (including civil disturbance in some cases) to show that they are disgruntled.

In general we are poor listeners. If you have been trained in listening skills you will know how hard it is to maintain your attentiveness and concentration and really listen to someone else (see Non-defensive listening, page 117).

Listening effectively ensures several things, among them:

a) It gives us a better chance of really hearing the other person's point of view, and in particular their cares and concerns.

b) It helps the listener still their 'inner voice'. It is impossible to listen effectively if we are adding our own interpretations and anticipating their motives and intentions. Focusing our attention fully on the other person ('listening deeply', as it has been called) means that we avoid the distraction of our own thoughts.

c) It helps us to remain objective because we are attending to something outside ourselves. This reduces the risk of being swamped by our emotions.[3]

Guiding principle number one is therefore to make sure we fully understand the other person's point of view. And that means listening to them and understanding their needs rather than our own interpretations of what they mean or our own needs. It is particularly powerful in dealing with difficult interpersonal relations because when we demonstrate that we are truly listening we engender respect and rapport. By showing that we are really working to understand we will be practising de-escalation and offering respect. If we do nothing else in a tense situation this will at least start to open up the lines of communication.

2. Maintain dignity and self-respect

When we are on the receiving end of somebody else's difficult behaviour it is not long before we start to harbour vengeful thoughts. Indeed, many of us are sustained by the thought that someday we can 'get even' with the other person. Unfortunately, such a point of view, deliciously seductive though it can be, will actually disempower us. This is because we become emotionally hooked into the process and are therefore less able to be objective about it. It's always important to retain a stance of dignity and self-respect, both with regard to ourselves and to the other person. Even though this is sometimes, indeed frequently, difficult to do, it is an essential prerequisite if we are going to be able to handle other people's difficult behaviour constructively and positively.

Things will always turn out better when we actively work to protect the dignity and self-respect of the other party as well as ourselves. Remember that oppressive relationships rely on depersonalisation of the oppressed by the oppressor. Whether we are talking about bullying, dictatorships, wars (even those between 'democratic' nations), slavery or an abusive marriage, being able to successfully harm the other person requires that we first deny them their identity as a thinking, feeling member of the human race.

Conversely, it is much more difficult to be unpleasant when we start to see our 'enemy' as a real person, with all that implies. When dealing with people we find difficult, it is a natural human trait (and probably one dictated by nature for the survival of the species) to label those we see as our adversaries. Propagandists and military leaders have long made use of this, denigrating the 'enemy' in a way that disguises their real identity behind a façade of caricature, nicknames and stereotypes. Groups of people reduced to 'Charlie', 'Fritz' or 'Tommy' are stripped of their identities and easier to regard as a foe. Testimony from the First World War shows how ordinary people sometimes see through this.

A wartime truce

The conciliatory effect of seeing our adversary as human is illustrated by the story of the spontaneous Christmas truce between British and German troops during the First World War. As legend (backed by historical fact) has it, the opposing sides, miserably dug into their trenches in the fields of Flanders on 24 December 1914, were so moved to hear each other singing Christmas carols that they climbed out of their hideouts to meet in no-man's land, exchange gifts and even enjoy a game of football. This story is well supported by newspaper reports of the day on both sides, and subsequent interviews by historical researchers. The events occurred in several places at once and are said to have included both officers and troops. There are also records of similar events involving other nationalities. The sense of astonishment at the 're-humanising' of the enemy is immediately summed up in the words of Gunner Herbert Smith, one of the men who was there. 'The

German I met had been a waiter in London and could use our language a little. He says he didn't want to fight and I think he was telling the truth... I know this statement takes some believing but it is absolutely correct. Fancy a German shaking your flapper as though he were trying to smash your fingers and a few days later trying to plug you. I hardly knew what to think about it...'

Needless to say, such fraternisation, though apparently tolerated to some extent by the officers on the ground, was considered tantamount to treason by the High Command and promptly banned since quite obviously it threatened the continuation of the war.

The WWI example is the best known[4], but there are other examples of similar 'truces' occurring spontaneously over the last few hundred years.

To counter our natural tendency to depersonalise difficult people it is useful to actively adopt a stance designed to respect the integrity and dignity of the other person. This does not mean that we have to like them or their views, but, as any negotiator knows, we must respect their right to hold those views. Lawyer and mediator Brian Muldoon says, 'It is not necessary to agree or sympathise with our enemy, but it is foolish not to understand him.'[5]

I know that some people are uneasy with this idea, and that others will say they agree while keeping their fingers crossed behind their back. However, my reason for including this as one of the guiding principles is not because I want to rehash some sort of spiritual message about loving our enemies, but for the much more persuasive reason that it makes us more effective in dealing with them. It serves as a way for us to control our own emotional reactions, helping us look beyond our own prejudices and opinions. This is a necessary first step if we want to be effective in our dealings with difficult people.

3. Remember - people can't be changed

You might think this rather odd because of course people change. In fact, as a psychotherapist, and in my work in general, all my work is about change. People change and evolve throughout their lives. The point to keep in mind, though, is that any strategy which requires the other person to change in order to have satisfaction in a relationship is liable, in the short term, to pay off badly. When faced with pressure to change most self-respecting people dig their heels in. Therefore, any time we want to change somebody else's behaviour it is useful to remember that: it's the behaviour not the person which we are trying to change. As a codicil I would add that most of us would accept that we do something stupid occasionally, that our behaviour is sometimes inappropriate or ill-advised. Most of us would accept that on these occasions we could modify our behaviour to good effect. We might even accept help from colleagues or friends in doing this. It's the same when dealing with difficult behaviour. We are likely to get more mileage out of any strategy, in other words more positive results, when that strategy is aimed at changing the behaviour rather than the person.

True, people do change, but most of us do it when we are ready and in our own sweet time. Very few of us respond (even when it is someone close to us) by graciously thanking them for drawing our attention to what they see as our faults.

4. Express your own point of view

In any relationship, personal or professional, we must be free to express our own point of view. Indeed, when this is not possible, it indicates a relationship which is not functioning too well. One person will be dominating the relationship with the other unable or unwilling to express themselves or put their point of view forward. This means that in dealing with difficult behaviour we should of course allow the other person to express themselves, in an appropriate way, but that we too should be free to express our point of view.

Relationships that work well are symmetrical. They are balanced in such a way that each participant can express themselves freely and equally. Ideally, everyone should be able to express their views as they need to, and should be allowed equal time to do so. If you watch people in balanced conversations you will notice that their exchanges of speaking and listening roughly match in terms of the time spent on each. In tightly hierarchical systems, such as the military, these rules have not traditionally applied. Free debate is not encouraged for obvious reasons, though there are channels for an exchange of appropriate information. As a guiding principle in dealing with difficult behaviour, reminding ourselves that we must be free to express our point of view acts as a memory jogger. We need first to have reflected on just what that point of view is. By extension we should also be ready to seek out the other person's point of view.

5. Win the day, not the fight

When we feel we have been wronged, or that we are losing control, the focus is usually on short-term gain - surviving the argument, getting our own way or preventing ourselves from being treated unfairly. Adopting a longer-term view linked to our own personal development can be a source of energy and guidance that can help the decision-making process when handling difficult behaviour.

In real life

Verat had been at loggerheads with his colleague Virginia for several weeks, ever since he had been given extra responsibilities and a small raise. They worked for a publishing company, had shared an office for about two years and had previously got on well together. Then, Verat explained, things started to decline rapidly. 'From the day it was confirmed that I would be running the new project, Ginny started to act more coolly towards me. It was part of both our jobs to deal with the production department and in the past we had found it worked well to share information. We would update each other with relevant facts about the availability of production space, lead times and so forth. It soon got to a point where this was not happening. If I tried to give Ginny information she would ignore it and when I asked for her opinion, say, where so and so could be contacted this week, she simply replied with another question or a facetious comment.'

Verat tried building bridges with his colleague in the usual ways – by making positive gestures and offering help to Ginny when she was overloaded – all to no avail. 'I hung on for a time, waiting for her to get used to the idea that I had been promoted, though my change in position was really only symbolic since the increase in pay was not much,' said Verat. 'She seemed really jealous and I had to make a choice. I had already tried bringing things into the open and speaking about our differences so we could lay them to rest, but that hadn't worked, so I figured that I had three options: ignore it and get on with my work;   leave the job which I liked very much; or somehow let her think she had 'won' by letting her believe that my new responsibilities did not suit me. I was getting irritable and fed up and my sleep was suffering. The job was demanding and I knew that if it went on as it was I would end up making a serious mistake.' He chose the third option.

'The new project I had been given lasted about six months. Once it was successfully completed and I could add it to my CV, I arranged with my boss not to renew that part of my work. I did not really tell her why but I think she got my drift and from then on there were no new projects. It meant giving up a bit of prestige and the small bonuses I would have got from time to time, but it was more important to me to be able to get on with my work in a stress-free environment because I had my sights set on higher things.'

Verat chose the course he did because he wanted to build a successful career unhindered by personal disputes. 'I knew that I would either be promoted to a much better position or that I would be off to pastures new when it suited me. I did not want Ginny's behaviour, which I really didn't seem to be able to resolve or change, to wind up as a black mark on my employment record. Although I thought the whole thing was unfair, I reasoned that it was in my long-term interest to 'manage' the situation until I no longer had to work so closely with this person.'

Verat's example may get some people hopping mad, and even some of his colleagues felt he should not have 'backed down' as they saw it. But he believes he chose the right course. Having tried everything he knew to correct the situation – ignoring it had not worked and he didn't want to leave the job just yet – he decided to remove the reason for the apparent jealousy. 'We were never again as close as before,' he said later, 'but in a few weeks we were able to work efficiently together and I could get on with my life.' He was able to overcome his feelings of injustice or rancour because he had his sights fixed firmly on a longer-term target: promotion to a better job.

These guiding principles can act as a framework to structure any response you choose for dealing with awkward behaviour. I cannot claim they are entirely mine, because they have been around in various forms for thousands of years. People have told me that they act as a useful reminder and a way of doing a 'reality check' when they have been under pressure from a difficult person.

Chapter 4
Why are people difficult?

The Greek philosopher Epictetus said, 'It is not the things themselves that worry us, but the opinions that we have about those things.' Though he said this nearly 2,000 years ago cognitive therapists today work very much along the same lines; if we can change our beliefs (opinions) about events in our lives they have less control over us.

In dealing with difficult people it is very often our opinion of them – even though we may be perfectly justified in having it – which controls our responses. If I believe that someone is going to be unpleasant towards me (because they have been before), the chances are that I will be on the defensive straight away.

It follows that if we are not careful about how we arrive at our conclusion, our inclination will be to confirm our existing beliefs about the person, rather than to look for new information that might help us tackle their behaviour. This becomes more problematic when we cobble together beliefs based on even less reliable information, such as the way the person looks or, worse, someone else's opinion of them.

It is natural to jump to conclusions about things that might threaten us. Our brain has evolved in such a way as to give us a powerful 'short cut' in times of perceived danger. This is part of the package that Daniel Goleman calls 'Emotional Intelligence'.[1] In terms of the development of a species, the ability to make snap decisions to keep its members safe is a great resource; the vast majority of animals get through life mostly on this automatic pilot. But as Joseph LeDoux points out, 'Those animals that can readily switch from automatic pilot to wilful control have a tremendous extra advantage. This advantage depends on the wedding of emotional and cognitive functions'.[2] Our unconsciously driven response in any situation is to err on the side of caution. Left unchecked this will keep us safe – a great attribute if we were still living in the primitive stage of our evolutionary past – but we have also developed a thinking part of the mind that can mediate these responses; I can think before I act. At least, on a good day I do.

Mid-course corrections

Our unconscious responses are so powerful that this decision-making process is continuously being carried out unbeknown to us. We make thousands upon thousands of tiny adjustments in our daily lives based on the information we are receiving, without any conscious effort. These 'mid-course corrections', as I call them, include decisions like choosing the best moment to step off a kerb and cross a road to more instantaneous reflexes such as hitting a tennis ball or dodging a flying object. From the point of view of keeping safe, we are permanently conducting a continuous, subliminal risk assessment.

Most of the time this process goes unchallenged; this is just the way it is designed to work. Some things happen so quickly that there is not time to think about our response and even if there were, nature does not want us to interfere with a perfectly good safety device. Other situations are simply too routine for us to interrupt our day with conscious intervention: walking round, rather than under, a ladder for example. Still others – such as driving a car or making a pot of tea – we know so well that they consist almost entirely of a series of virtually automatic responses. Our repertoire of responses is a powerful ally without which we would probably soon perish. It has served us well throughout the aeons of our development on earth and continues to do so.

Life in the modern world, however, demands that we check some of our automatic reactions, if only to ensure that we get along with each other. These days life is much more complicated and we require a highly sophisticated set of responses to navigate our daily social interactions. We can override an instant dislike for someone else – for example, by shaking hands with them even though they may make our skin crawl, or by appearing calm and polite towards someone who has made us angry – in order to preserve social harmony (or keep our job).

Unfortunately, the process can work in reverse, so to speak. Rather than checking our emotional reaction as it happens and moderating our behaviour as we might see fit, we may only notice how we feel after the event. The natural response to this is to try and explain to ourselves why we feel as we do. I will respond to a 'threat' at an unconscious level and on noticing my response (or the other person's response to my response) I will start to search for an explanation.

The question of 'Why?'

For the unsuspecting there is a trap in asking the question, 'Why is this person difficult?' It raises a couple of issues that affect not only the answer, but the need to ask it at all.

The unsettling enquiry with which so many people attempt to assuage doubt in their lives is the question 'Why?' The belief that in order to solve a problem we first have to understand it is one of the great myths of westernised thinking.[3] It is so deeply embedded in us that it is generally unquestioned, but it causes untold misery. The 'opinions' that Epictetus speaks of are no more than explanations, and explanations are the result of our internal reflections. They are the stories we tell ourselves in the search for understanding. Up to a point this is fine, but it has serious limitations.

Imagine that you have just witnessed a striking or unusual event in public. Say, for example, that you notice a man in the checkout queue at the supermarket whose trolley contains nothing but several dozen pairs of women's tights. Or perhaps you spot a senior colleague at work, normally known for her sober and professional dress sense, crossing the car park dressed as a clown. The chances are that your first reaction is to try to find an explanation for the behaviour. Assuming that in neither case you feel like asking the person to explain the motives for their actions, it is likely that you will be wondering, 'Why are they doing that?'

We have such a pressing need to explain things to ourselves that in these situations the mind immediately starts generating rationalisations to satisfy the hunger of our curiosity: 'Maybe his wife is in prison', 'Perhaps he manages a women's football team' or some less charitable judgement about his lifestyle and habits, or 'She must be on her way to a fancy dress party'.

We use our experience and judgement to assess the situation and come up with a conclusion. Even though this is only a hypothesis generated by our thought processes (at least until we have it checked out with the person concerned or some other reliable source), it is a short step away from allowing our interpretation to become an explanation.

Now relate this same process to the actions of a difficult person. Somebody shouts at us in public, or a colleague repeatedly lets us down for some reason and naturally we are angry or put out. Once we have got over this emotional reaction and are able to think it through, we will try to make some sense of it. But in doing so we are more likely to find explanations for the behaviour than to make objective observations about it – focusing on the 'Why?' rather than the 'What?'

Since we are concerned here with the effects of difficult people's behaviour, we need to ask questions about what to do about it rather than why it is happening. 'Why?' speculates on cause whereas 'What?' relates to effect. In order to test the value of this, try asking 'Why does it rain?' compared to 'What happens when it rains?', then check the usefulness of the answer in deciding how to deal with rain. Asking why things happen is all very well if you are a philosopher (or a meteorologist in the example above), and if you have time to speculate on the cause. It is less useful when you want to generate action to deal with an effect.[4]

We are unconsciously guided by culturally bound cause-and-effect thinking: a process which is so powerful that until our attention is drawn to it we can unwittingly set a course which will lead us on to the rocks. Speculating on the causes for someone's behaviour and trying to find some explanation for it can paralyse us; we stymie our own ability to deal with it by our own mental processes.

'Thinking,' says Guy Claxton, visiting professor of psychology and education at Bristol University, 'can get in the way of a whole variety of mental functions, including everyday memory and decision-making as well as intuition and insight'.[5]

We have all known times in our lives when we have got caught in a self-defeating loop of analysis. 'Paralysis by analysis', as it is known, can happen when we turn something over and over in our minds with such regularity that our ruminations seemed to develop a life of their own. It is intuitive to ask 'Why?' in order to attempt to understand the reasons for something going wrong. But this line of inquiry is not a lot of help in dealing with a difficult person since it only provides speculative information and does little to help us decide on our course of action.

Interpretations or observations?

Interpretations come from the observer, not the person or thing being observed (in this case the person causing the trouble). Observations, on the other hand, report on what is actually witnessed – visible actions and behaviour – in a given situation. Any interpretation, even one based on knowing someone for many years, is really only a form of guessing. There are many experts out there ready to tell us why people do what they do, this is part of the Freudian and scientific legacy that has led us to believe there is a body of knowledge (in this case psychology) that contains reliable explanations for people's behaviour. Unfortunately, this is not so.

Over the past 150 years psychology has provided millions

of textbooks on human behaviour. It is a rich and fascinating topic and a vitally useful field of study, and we should not seek to diminish its importance in any way. What we must remember in dealing with other people's behaviour, however, is that there are around 250 models of my own discipline, psychotherapy, and many, many more belief systems under the broad heading of psychology. Anyone familiar with even part of this vast area of study will confirm that it contains so much conflicting information that the only thing we can really be certain about is that nobody really knows why people act as they do. This valuable body of knowledge provides a framework for thinking about the actions and reactions of human beings, but it should not be taken as some sort of doctrinal system for explaining why people act as they do. Good psychology, like any other field of scientific enquiry, sticks to observable facts. Theorising about why something happens has its place, but only as a starting point. As Einstein said, 'A theory can be proved by experiment; but no path leads from experiment to the birth of a theory.'[6] Robert Louis Stevenson also noted, 'When the torrent sweeps a man against a boulder, you must expect him to scream, and you need not be surprised if the scream is sometimes a theory.'[7]

Incidentally, it is worth remembering that psychology grew out of the field of philosophy and that until William James published his Principles of Psychology in 1891, the subject never really existed as a separate field of inquiry.[8] Indeed, James himself was a philosopher as well as a scientist who had studied widely in Europe with many of the leading thinkers of the day before returning to his native America, where he published his influential work. Having given the world his highly perceptive and visionary thoughts on psychology James later returned to his first love, philosophy.[9]

Since time began the main preoccupation of philosophers has been to make life more meaningful by offering interpretations of things. It was and still is the job of philosophers to know how to conduct an inquiry. In the words of Lou Marinoff, philosophy professor at the City College of

New York, 'We don't give you answers but help you ask profitable questions.'[10]

One of the ways we have been taught to respond to things we don't like – in this case difficult behaviour – is to use a line of questioning which grew out of philosophical inquiry. This was designed precisely to explain those things in life that generally could not be changed nor explained in any other way – the thoughts, emotions and feelings that people experience and that affect their conduct. It has been particularly valuable in helping people down the ages to deal with paradox: those unsettling instances where contradictory ideas or facts seem inseparable, for example, 'Why does a good God allow bad things to happen?' It has always been a vitally important job (although history is full of examples of philosophers who have had to flee their countries, suffer imprisonment or even been executed for their views), but it was never intended to produce answers to questions like, 'How can I get John to stop insulting me?' (Though it could help with the question 'How can I learn to live with someone who insults me?')[11]

The second and more powerful argument for avoiding this introspective approach is that interpretations of people's behaviour go hand-in-hand with judgements, and when we make a judgement we immediately start to disempower ourselves. Cause-and-effect thinking is again at the bottom of this.

Why ask 'Why?' so often?

The problem with this question, when we ask it of ourselves, is that the answers are quite literally a figment of our own imagination. If we really want to know why somebody does something, surely the best idea would be to ask them. Critics of this approach will immediately raise the objections that:

- people very often don't know why they do what they do
- even when they do know they frequently won't tell us

- any educated person knows that human drives and
motivations are so deeply embedded in the unconscious
that they are unavailable to us when examining our own
behaviour (a more intellectual version of the first point).

There is certainly some truth in these points, but 150 years
of psychology has taught us that guessing at why people do
what they do is almost always a lousy way to go about things.
Even the highly sophisticated art of offender profiling, a
branch of forensic psychology made famous by the *Cracker*
series on television, is only a form of intelligent guessing,
backed up with some specific and very detailed observations at
the scene of the crime. All deductions are based on clues that
the investigators can elicit from the traces left by the offender
or the victim. Theorising about motives is discouraged in
favour of a thorough examination of the forensic evidence.

Brent Turvey, a forensic scientist and criminal profiler who
advises the legal and mental health communities, said in a
detailed explanation of the techniques used, 'Due to this
thoroughness, *learned or experiential generalizations can be kept
from obscuring or misleading investigations.*' He went on to explain
just why such rigour is so vital for accuracy: 'Investigators with
a lot of years on the job, or a lot of experience investigating a
particular type of crime, tend to formulate theories about a
case early on. Instead of investigating the case, they may instead
spend their efforts attempting to prove a theory. Deductive
Criminal Profiling precludes theory generation, and
subsequent bruised egos, *until a full investigative analysis* has
been done' (my italics in both cases).[12]

Similarly, when dealing with difficult people, we need to
resist our natural inclination to look for motives and offer
interpretations for their behaviour. However good our
deductive reasoning, we cannot be sure of the accuracy of our
conclusions.

If we want to work with or round difficult behaviour, it is
helpful to look for information about the nature and context
of the behaviour, rather than wrestling with endless

interpretations of the person's innermost drives. This is easier if we drop the question 'Why?' and replace it with 'What makes people difficult?'

A powerful reason for adopting this approach is that when we start making interpretations of other people's behaviour we automatically start attributing cause where it is more useful to look at effect. When we start looking for a cause as an explanation it is a very short step to personalising their behaviour so that we are likely to attribute it to some essential flaw in their character. Personalising in this way is risky because it threatens objectivity. Judgements tend to suspend our reasoning ability. In the words of S.I. Hayakawa, 'The worrying thing about judgements is the temporary blindness they induce.' [13]

Clearly we need some interpretations to get through life, but I want to make it clear that:

- any conclusions drawn at this point are only guesses about why the other person acts as they do
- it is a short step from interpreting another person's behaviour to attributing motives to their actions
- this can lead to making a judgement about the person which limits our ability to see things clearly.

The behaviour, not the person

Generally we are very fond of who we are and don't want to change. The same goes for those around us, and difficult people in particular. People invest a huge amount of energy in staying just the way they are and don't take kindly to attempts to change them. On the other hand, we may have a little more luck if we try and change their behaviour. As I have mentioned already, the aim of the game is to get more productive outcomes with difficult people. Identifying the behaviour, rather than the person, as the nuisance factor in the equation depersonalises any comments we may make. Identifying the behaviour also helps to empower us since it reduces the likelihood of blame.

Separating the person from the problem

In real life

When Peter returned home one Monday evening his three-year-old daughter proudly showed him a great piece of artwork she had done while he was at work. Her beautiful drawing – which stretched round two walls of the living room – had been done using one of those fat, black marker pens. Peter had only finished decorating the walls the previous day. Naturally, as a proud and loving father, he praised her artistic abilities. They discussed how she managed to reach so high – she had walked across the back of the settee – and various other details as she led him round the mural to get a better look. He then pointed out that the next time she felt like doing a drawing or picture, that it might be more appropriate if she were to use a piece of paper (or at least if she must do it on the wall, please use the piece of wall that mummy had decorated!).

Peter did not identify the behaviour with the child by accusing his daughter of being bad or wrong. In explaining to her that the drawing was done in the wrong place he was identifying the actions rather than the person as the target for change. Of course, we all know this, but we start to forget it when children grow into adults.

Think about somebody who has done something recently that you did not like. Say they have 'borrowed' something of yours without asking your permission and when they brought it back it had been damaged in some way. Or perhaps they are obstructing you somehow in your daily life or work. Whatever it is, it should be something that rankles you a little. Take a moment to think about the irritating aspects of this person and their actions. Now, make a conscious effort to step back from the situation and identify the behaviour involved. Rather than thinking about not liking the person for what they have done, ask yourself which aspects of their *behaviour* (their actions) have caused the problem.

When most people do this exercise they notice a perceptual shift. They feel differently about the situation when they examine the aspects of the behaviour they don't like rather than thinking about the person and their actions together. This is a fundamental point when dealing with difficult people. (See also Separating Impact from Intent, page 189.)

If you have trouble doing this exercise, and find that you are unable to separate the person from the problem, the chances are that you are simply too emotionally aroused by the event. In other words, you are still too mad at them!

Separating the 'What?' from the 'Why?' can be a powerful and liberating step to take because it allows us to remain more objective about the situation and to make choices undistorted by a need to get even, blame or punish.

Before planning how we can tackle difficult behaviour, there are some useful questions to ask ourselves first. For example, is the behaviour a personal response to a potentially threatening situation? Is the behaviour specific to a particular time, place or individual? Is it due to a lack of social or personal skills, or could it be induced by stress?

It may be self-defence

We can all think of situations where uncertainty, doubt or feeling uncomfortable has made us irascible, argumentative, withdrawn or uncooperative. It is predictable that when we enter a situation that we find challenging or uncomfortable we can become difficult ourselves. Our natural response – unless we do something to control it – is to slip into one of four predetermined 'default modes' when we feel under threat (see the Satir Categories, page 92).

When confronted by someone else's difficult behaviour it is always a good idea to consider whether they may be expressing their own emotional responses to the situation: uncertainty, feeling out of control, fear, doubt, anxiety or whatever. We may not be able to do much about it, but this understanding can inform our behaviour towards them.

For example, I once saw a close colleague act in a way that made me angry and ashamed. We had been collaborating for several months on the same project and I had come to know him as someone who was calm, reasonable and not prone to emotional outbursts. When we went abroad to complete the final phase of the project, I was shocked to notice a dramatic change in his behaviour in the workplace. In doing his job as an instructor he became bombastic, aggressive and demeaning towards those he was supposed to be training. I did nothing about this immediately (to have intervened during the outburst would only have made matters worse). Instead, I waited until the working day was over and then, conversationally, brought the subject up, having first prepared the ground. I said something like, 'You know, Steve, I have always been impressed by how cool you are under pressure when we were working back at head office. In fact, I wished I could be more like you in that respect. You seemed to take everything in your stride and it was never too much trouble for you to help a colleague out.' This was all true, he had been chosen to accompany me abroad precisely because of his unflappability. Then I tackled him about his outbursts that day: 'I was really surprised to see this new side to you, what was all that about?'

Steve replied that he knew it had been out of character, but that he had extensive experience of the kind of culture in which we were working (we were in Russia at the time) and that this was his usual way of working. He conceded, though, that he had been nervous about how the trainees would respond to him and had perhaps 'gone over the top a bit'.

I acknowledged that he had far greater experience than me in this area, and said that I too had been nervous in anticipation of our reception. But I also went on to say that his behaviour had embarrassed me and, I believed, would harm his reputation with the trainees if it continued. As well as that, I reminded him that we were representatives both of our organisation and our country.

To his credit, Steve took this on board and became one of the most well-liked members of the 12-strong team working on the project.

Very often, what we perceive as difficult behaviour in somebody else may simply be their response to a stressful situation. Perhaps they are floundering, out of their depth, or unsure of the appropriate way to act. For example, staff may watch a perfectly agreeable, empathetic colleague become overbearing, bombastic and apparently uncaring when they are promoted to a management position.

In cases like this, an empathetic approach is probably best in the first instance. I would not suggest using words like 'insecurity' or 'uncertainty' or any other language that suggested you were trying to analyse the person. Simply approach the subject as non-confrontationally as possible by putting them at their ease and discussing their behaviour. The main thing to remember is that, if it is some sort of defence mechanism, you will have to choose your moment, the setting and your words extremely carefully to avoid witnessing more of the same defensive behaviour.

It may be context-specific

We all find some situations more difficult than others. Some people hate the dentist's or the doctor's waiting room, others don't like speaking in front of a group. We also all have our little idiosyncrasies and prejudices. If you need to tackle someone's difficult behaviour consider that the context may have something to do with it. Steve's outbursts in Russia may partly have been to compensate for his nervousness, but they were also directly connected to the environment. As he told me, 'This is how I am when I work in Russia'. If you have to deal with someone's bad behaviour in a public waiting area, consider moving them away from the audience first. Just as their bad behaviour will have been witnessed by others, so will your attempts to deal with them. The person may feel they have to 'perform' in front of the crowd and if so, it will more difficult to calm them down. You also run the risk, if the behaviour gets out of control, of the crowd becoming difficult as well. Suddenly you could find you have to deal with a whole group of difficult people. Discussing matters in a different environment could change the situation.

But difficult behaviour may also be more personal. What if the person is only like that with you? Check to see if other colleagues or friends experience the same response. If they don't, what are they doing that works? I often go to organisations where staff regularly have to deal with conflict and disagreement. One of my first questions is to ask who doesn't have a problem (or has less of a problem). I want to identify the staff members who have the least difficulty with their client group. There is usually at least one person who comes out relatively unscathed or handles things in such a way that they get less aggravation. These people are a resource in the organisation. It may be that they have better interpersonal skills than others, more time or some other gift (humour, for example) which means that, with them, fewer people are difficult. Comparing responses may point to how to change the context of the behaviour in order to reduce the chances of conflict.

Ground crews at airports, doctors' receptionists, call centre staff and veterinary inspectors visiting abattoirs during the BSE crisis are just some of the groups I have worked with, helping them deal more effectively with difficult behaviour. There are many more examples of situations which, by their very nature, put people under stress. Tempers can flare or people can become uncooperative in some other way. Loss of power, uncertainty and fear of authority can all be linked to the context in which people find themselves. In such cases, particularly when dealing with clients, service users or the public, there may be something that could be done at an organisational level to alleviate the problem.

One such case was a small cinema where the box office staff frequently had to bear the brunt of angry patrons, since the venue was not large and was often sold out. People would come in, eagerly anticipating seeing the film of their choice – and the only one showing as it was a single-screen cinema – only to be told that it was full. The result would be frequent rows with angry members of the public. When I asked why the box office staff had to deal with this I was told, 'Because they are the ones who have to give the bad news.' The cinema manager had never thought of putting a board outside the cinema saying 'Sold out'. Doing so would surely have reduced the number of surprised and disappointed people that the box office staff had to deal with.

It may be due to lack of skills

In real life

Jason grew up in a fairly normal lower middle-class home. He was part of a loving family of parents, two sisters and himself. He told me that throughout his childhood and adolescence he could never remember his parents having an argument. The children occasionally heard raised voices behind closed doors or had to submit to long periods of frosty silence during mealtimes, but they never actually got to see their parents arguing.

The reason that Jason and I were speaking about this was that he had come to consult me about the terrible arguments he and his wife were having. The problem was that he did not know how to argue!

'It started a few days after we got married,' he told me. 'Mostly it was about nothing at all, she would just flare up and no matter what I did she wouldn't calm down.'

When I asked Jason what he had tried he said that he remained calm and 'above it all'. 'I wasn't going to come down to her level', he said.

Leaving aside for the moment Jason's unfortunate choice of words – it would probably enflame the most mild-mannered of us to be told that we were functioning at a low level – I wanted to know how he viewed domestic strife in general. His response was that he didn't see the need for arguing if you loved someone. After all, he said, 'My parents never argued and they were definitely a loving couple.' If it was Jason's belief that loving couples didn't argue, it might also be that arguments spelt danger. 'Exactly', he said, 'I thought if we are arguing like this so soon after getting married we must have made a terrible mistake. I could see it all ending in disaster.'

Jason was skills-deficient. In his model of the world, loving couples did not argue. He felt unsafe because he didn't know that it is possible to argue with someone you love and then kiss and make up.

It may be stress-induced

Stress can bring out the worst in us. Much of the behaviour in others which we experience as 'difficult' is really nothing more than them responding to the stressors in their lives.

The term 'stress' is much over-used these days, which means that its significance and consequences are often misunderstood or ignored. The term describes a constellation of physical and mental responses experienced by all of us when we perceive ourselves to be under pressure. Everyone will respond differently to a given stressor. For example, many people find public speaking a highly stressful event. Standing in front of an audience produces the full range of effects: racing pulse, dry mouth, trembling and total inability to remember their lines. Some of us, on the other hand, although we get a little stage fright before the big event, are able to function quite normally under the 'pressure' of the public eye. Whether this is because we have got used to it or because something in our make-up means that we experience a stimulating challenge where others feel a threat is neither here nor there. The point is that we all respond differently to a given stimulus; it is not stressful events that are the problem, it is how we respond to them. And how we respond will depend on individual make-up.

This is not to say that when we experience the adverse effects of stress we are somehow weak or faulty. I think the opposite is true. The stress response has been built into all animals for survival purposes. One thing we can be sure of is that when we develop stress-related symptoms (see the section on stress in the next chapter), our body is trying to tell us something. The problem comes when we either ignore or don't notice the early warning signs, our stress levels build up and this affects our behaviour (and eventually our health). The result in any system which is subjected to constant or extreme pressure is a breakdown or failure or disruption of the system in some way.

When someone is under pressure, difficult behaviour may result. This is worth bearing in mind when thinking about how to respond to their behaviour. We can all think of times when – because something we found stressful was going on – we were not able to take in new information or act in our normal, well-balanced way. Reminding ourselves how people can respond when they are under pressure is useful because it depersonalises their behaviour (they are responding to the circumstances, not us). It also provides hints as to some of the things we can do to work round the difficult behaviour if it is wholly or partly the result of stress. The behaviour shown by Steve earlier in this chapter is an example of this.

Responding constructively

Later in the book you will see that I have categorised difficult behaviour under seven different headings (see Chapter 8). This does not mean I am suggesting that we can fit the 60 million or so people in the British Isles into seven categories. Such an approach would be preposterous. The reason I have grouped some of the more common – one might say 'typical' – difficult characters under headings in this way is to provide a means of demonstrating ideas about how to respond constructively to them. They are rightly called 'characters' since they consist of scripts; they are not real people and, although many delegates at my seminars have told me they recognise them, I do not encourage you to start identifying people as 'Steamrollers' or 'Guerrillas'. Like any labels, they are intended to be descriptive and to provide a vehicle for illustrating techniques rather than a prescription for how to act.

Before turning to them, please read and consider the few basic principles I have outlined in this chapter. They will help you stay on track and avoid the common pitfalls of dealing with difficult behaviour. They will also help ensure that your interactions remain healthy, respectful and balanced.

I have found over the years that three other factors play a key role when people have decided to adopt a particular course of action. While these are the sort of things most of us would mentally review before undertaking any project, we frequently fail to do so in our relationships.

The three Cs

Before embarking on any strategy to modify somebody else's behaviour, I think it is important to focus on our own intentions and desired outcomes and also to think about the level of commitment we will need to implement our chosen strategy. This is why I came up with the three Cs. These stand for Context, Cost, and Commitment.

In real life

Michael felt the interview went well. He had already been excited by the idea of the job he was applying for, and the other details given during the interview simply confirmed this. Fortunately he didn't have to wait long for the committee's decision; they had been impressed by him, too, and were keen for him to start.

Michael was to run a new project in the voluntary sector for an existing organisation. 'I had a pretty free rein, particularly in the early days when my brief was to research what other similar services were already available in the area, and to set up a liaison group to share information.

'I was stunned the first time my boss came striding into my office and set about what I can only call ranting. I could not really get the point of it, but he was clearly very angry about something. This then became a pattern; he would do it several times a week.'

Context

First let's consider the context in which the difficult behaviour happens. In the escalator rage example in Chapter 2, even though it occurred in a public place, it was a one-off and George was unlikely ever to meet the protagonist again. The amount of time and effort that would be required for dealing with this is likely to be different from the example above where Michael has to regularly deal with his manager's ugly behaviour. You can see that the contexts of the two situations are quite different.

Cost

If the contexts are different, then the likely cost will also be different. The cost to George in the escalator story was light. Even if he did nothing, the personal cost to him was not very high. Contrast that with Michael's example, where the cost of having an angry and resistant colleague confronting him on a regular basis is very much higher. It will cause stress, aggravation, possible sleepless nights and a whole range of other intrusive factors. The employer will also suffer costs in that Michael would not be working at his best while distracted by the problem, which could lead to expensive mistakes in the workplace.

Commitment

Having thought about the context and the cost, we next need to think about the level of commitment we will need to tackle the difficult behaviour. Again, to use the escalator example, the level of commitment that George required was minimal. It was a one-off, and although his chosen strategy didn't work – well, no harm done, he simply went on his way. Just as the cost of such an interaction is not high nor will be the degree of commitment needed to sort it out.

On the other hand, let's consider somebody who has to deal with a ranting boss on a regular basis, like Michael. Let's assume that this member of staff takes the problem to their boss's boss, explaining that they are having difficulty working with their boss because of their overbearing behaviour, as Lois did in Chapter 1. Unfortunately, as we have seen, the senior manager, far from assuming any responsibility or offering help in the situation, simply said that she would have to 'toughen up' if she wanted to stay working for the firm, because that's how it was in that organisation. Leaving aside the veiled threat 'if she wanted to stay working', this quite clearly puts the problem, and the responsibility for solving it, back on Lois' shoulders. In this case the cost to her was very high (she had daily contact with some very nasty behaviour) and furthermore it seems that it was endemic in the organisation. The level of commitment she would need to tackle it would therefore also be high. Not only would she have to sort out the manager concerned and learn to work with their behaviour in some more constructive way, she might also need to challenge the attitude of the whole organisation. Faced with such an entrenched problem, Lois seriously had to review the resources and energy available to her. She would need to be highly motivated, have good support elsewhere in the organisation and good family support outside. She would need to be confident that, with determination, she could handle the behaviour. As we have already seen, Lois decided that it was not feasible and to look elsewhere for work.

In looking at Context, Cost and Commitment we need to balance these various factors before embarking on any course of action. No two situations are the same and our strategy should take this into account. The three Cs will help us evaluate our position sensibly and with a degree of balance.

Observation rather than interpretation

I started this chapter with the question I am always asked in radio interviews, "Why are people difficult?", and I have explained why I think this question can be so unproductive. Searching for motives and reasons is a natural response if we are on the receiving end of difficult behaviour, but it is of limited value. Partly this is because we can only speculate on causes and partly because, once we make a judgement, it is easy to start attributing blame. Judgements also severely curtail our objectivity. Understanding the importance of asking the right questions is a good start, and it is also important to recognise the limitations of any explanations we come up with by this process. Observing the behaviour and checking it out – directly or indirectly – is likely to be more fruitful (and certainly more accurate) than guessing and interpreting.

Nevertheless, we must consider some of the contributory factors that generate difficult behaviour. I have provided a nominal overview rather than a complete list. Of the points not covered here I should point out that difficult behaviour may also be an expression of some very real problem in the other person's life, including physical or emotional pain, dramatic life events or suffering in some way. There is a virtually unlimited list of potential causes, because any time we get upset or are uncertain we can become difficult. The point of this chapter was simply to identify some ways to avoid being drawn into a self-defeating pattern of behaviour when dealing with it.

The following chapter explores how we humans behave under pressure that we find stressful, and some of the social implications, particularly in the workplace. One often-overlooked body of research concerns the differing physiological and cognitive responses of men and women. Gender equality at work is one of society's more noble aspirations. But that is all it is; men and women are about as equal as peaches and walnuts when it comes to behaviour. And it is the very differences we ignore that can cause so much trouble and lead to some of us being labelled difficult when all we are doing is responding as nature designed us to do.

Chapter 5
Stress, emotion, gender and confusion

Most of us can function pretty well under pressure when we feel we have some degree of control over events or can determine our response to the demands being made upon us. However, when we feel that those demands or expectations exceed our ability to deliver what is being asked of us, we start to become stressed.

'Stress' is perfectly natural and necessary. It is a generalised term for what is simply the body's reaction to extra demands being made on it. It is only harmful when these demands become excessive or constant. Conversely, life without stimulation can be as damaging as life with too much.

Human beings are creative, adaptable and tenacious creatures. We are capable of surprising even ourselves with our successes. We thrive on a challenge, something that gives us a sense of purpose and achievement, even when it involves an element of risk. Some high achievers will even tell you that it is *because* of the risk – and the 'buzz' that they feel afterwards – that they are attracted to, say, mountaineering or Arctic exploration. The explorer Sue Stockdale, who walked 350 miles through Arctic wastes to reach the magnetic North Pole in 1996 (the first British woman to do so), told me: 'The more the risk, the greater the sense of achievement, and your confidence grows as a result.' She added that an element of uncertainty is part of the attraction: 'So often I've said to myself in extreme moments, "If I'd known it would be this bad I'd never have done it". The unknown adds excitement.'

Any challenge produces a certain amount of stress, fear, uncertainty and fatigue in the participants before they know the final payoff. When our efforts are channelled to some end and we feel in control – even though there may be some risk involved – we flourish, it builds self-esteem and confidence, and the result is better emotional and physical health.

Because stress in itself is not detrimental, some authors speak of good stress and bad stress. Hans Selye, whose pioneering work half a century ago established the field of stress research, spoke of Eustress, to describe positive, challenging experiences of stress which lead to higher expectations, versus Distress, the result of disappointment, threat, failure, embarrassment or other negative experiences. Cognitive neuroscientist Michael Gazzaniga coined the terms controllable and uncontrollable stress to explain how stressful events can have a positive or a negative effect on us depending on how we perceive them.[1] The crucial point here is that the more we feel in control the less likely stress is to affect us badly.

In real life

During the 1980s I was working in Paris for a company involved in preparing tenders for the renewal of resources in the USSR (as it was then). I was heading a team whose job it was to put together the right mix of technical equipment and expertise for each project, and then to supervise installation of the equipment and to ensure any relevant staff training. This involved intricate and protracted negotiations with the Russians to decide whether the package being offered by the French company actually responded to the Russians' needs. Like any such exercise the process involved huge quantities of written information which had to accompany the discussions. Preparations for the hundred or so kilos of paperwork that had to accompany the negotiators to Moscow for each stage of the process would start several months in advance. Even so, for the final week before the departure date of any negotiating team, it would be all hands to the pumps (or in this case, the photocopiers) to ensure that everything was finished on time.

It was accepted that two or three times a year, everyone in the office would work night and day reproducing all the necessary documentation. Writers, technicians, translators, secretaries – everyone regardless of rank or status would work side by side, round the clock. We organised ourselves into three shifts and normal office routines and protocols were abandoned to make sure that everything was finished on time. We all worked longer than the eight hours on our allotted shift, we took it in turns to eat and sleep when we could. I lived close to the office so could nip home for a few hours' sleep when necessary, others were not so lucky and some people even slept on the floor so that they would not have to waste any time in travelling. It was demanding, hectic and exhilarating. There would be minor squabbles, occasional tears, lots of laughter and as much coffee as you could drink. When the deadline came, the negotiating team would leave Paris for Moscow and all the other office-based staff would return to their normal routines; within 24 hours there would be no sign of the previous week to ten days' clamour and disruption.

The curious thing about this whole exercise was that though it was an immensely stressful event for all concerned (several people would have lost their jobs if we had missed the deadline and we all suffered disruption to our family lives and routines), it was seen as an exhilarating and exciting event: the challenge had to be met. Frayed tempers, late translations, broken photocopiers, missing pages – there were any number of obstacles and delays to be overcome. But the team rose to meet them and stress was never even mentioned. Everyone involved believed (most of the time) that we could meet the demands being made on us and the challenge motivated and vitalised the team.

The people in the Paris office in this story were undoubtedly under stress, "running on adrenalin" as we say, but this was not doing any harm. On the contrary, it was an enjoyable experience for the staff. The significant factors are: we were all there by choice; there was a clear point to what we were doing; we were working towards a specific and achievable deadline; the results we obtained were measurable; our efforts were recognised by others; the timescale was finite in that the 'emergency' was short term; and there was an element of novelty.

Contrast this story with a typical modern workplace scenario. Stress at work is caused when the factors above do not apply. Staff are often told when and where to work (no choice); do not understand the aim of what they are doing (no point); demands on them and consequently the pressure are ongoing (no specific deadline); the results of their work are frequently vague or invisible (not measurable); acknowledgement or praise for their efforts is generally lacking (unrecognised by others); 'emergencies' are constant (no end in sight); and the work is often repetitive or boring (monotony rather than novelty).

These types of stressors produce a working environment that brings out the worst in people, and where difficult behaviour can thrive.

Stress and physiology

It is a truism that life today is stressful, and to some extent it always has been. This is why we – and every other species of mammal on the planet – evolved with a set of responses for dealing with stressful situations. Known collectively as the fight-or-flight response, these automatic reactions have evolved to keep us alive. Our primitive ancestors, it is assumed, faced physical threat on a daily basis. In order to deal with an attack by a wild beast or some other emergency, they needed to be physically equipped in an instant (since that is how such emergencies usually occur) for defence or rapid departure. Any threat automatically triggers a whole constellation of physiological changes in preparation of the anticipated exertion involved: stress hormones are instantly secreted into the system; fat dissolves to produce more available forms of energy; cells throughout the body and the liver deliver glucose which is pumped by the blood to the main muscle groups to fuel the action (at the expense of other, non-essential, functions such as digestion, tissue repair and fighting infection); breathing quickens; muscles tense; pupils dilate and our thinking style changes as we become more alert to the threat and ready for action.

This is a system that has served us well in moments of crisis throughout our history and continues to do so. But the nature of the stressors (threats) we encounter in modern times is different from those our ancestors were equipped for. Not many of us face the risk of likely death or physical injury in our daily lives, and for those that do, the hostile conditions are generally limited to specific situations or circumstances: war, mugging or some accidental or natural catastrophe, for example. The fight-or-flight response is still as necessary as ever, however, since it is specifically intended for rapid reactions to short-term events.

For most of us, though, the situations and crises we face in our daily lives do not actually threaten our physical survival. Arguing with a spouse or preparing for an exam can be highly stressful but in most cases they are not likely to kill or maim us. The sort of challenging life events which threaten us these days, such as moving house, getting the sack or even losing a loved one, are not in the same league – in terms of the survival of the species – as the stressors our ancestors had to deal with. This is not to minimise such trials and tragedies, nor am I ignoring the very real dangers from physical attack that still exist in the world today. The fact remains that the things that stress us most often and, more to the point, switch us into fight-or-flight mode, are the daily events that do not require an extreme survival response.

Yet any situation where we feel endangered will trigger this response and its associated emotions of anger – it does not take visibly impending danger to start things off. Daniel Goleman, author of the hugely influential book *Emotional Intelligence*, says: 'Endangerment can be signalled not just by an outright physical threat but also, as is more often the case, by a symbolic threat to self-esteem or dignity: being treated unjustly or rudely, being insulted or demeaned, being frustrated in pursuing an important goal.'[2]

How many of the encounters with difficult people you have come across in your life do you think this description fits? How many times have you found yourself reacting to 'being treated unjustly or rudely, being insulted or demeaned or being frustrated in pursuing an important goal', as Goleman puts it? Most people respond like typical human beings – and just as nature intended – our bodies react to the 'threat' with the stress arousal response I described above.

Chronic stress...

Another significant aspect linked to life in the modern world, compared with the one our early ancestors inhabited, is that today we are far more likely to endure threats to our well-being which last longer than the typical Neanderthal-being-chased-by-a-tiger routine. The type of stress caused by the ever-present pressures of modern life affects our health and the way we behave, and it may be at the root of much of the difficult behaviour we have to deal with, especially at work.

Chronic stress describes the effects on the human body of stressors that don't go away after a few hours or days. The sinister aspect to chronic stress is that the changes in physical and mental functioning brought about by the fight-or-flight response – changes which were intended to be temporary – start to become more permanent, affecting our health and the way we reason.

The long-term effects of chronic stress on the human

organism are well documented.[3] Helped by press coverage of high-profile cases fought and won by stressed staff suing their employers, armies of stress management specialists and the determined efforts of unions, some voluntary organisations and eventually the government, the importance of the topic has been raised. Even so, misunderstanding of the syndrome is still widespread. It is viewed with suspicion by many organisations I come into contact with[4] and, judging by the poor response of most employers to the stress sustained by many of their staff (and indeed, our own failure as individuals to understand and do something constructive about reducing the stress in our lives and the lives of those we love), we still do not take it seriously. [5]

The other disturbing factor is that chronic stress is not just caused by obviously stressful events such as the threat of redundancy, the pressures of commuting or striving to meet impossible deadlines. Studies have shown that our position in the social hierarchy can also influence how stress affects us. It has been understood by anthropologists for some time that primates, who like ourselves live in social groups, have a strict set of rules about who has privileges and who does not. More recently, the work of neuroscientist Robert Sapolsky, based on his studies of baboons in Africa, has shown that the exacting social hierarchies that are a feature of their lives cause considerable stress to the members of the lower orders. The chronic effects of being 'kept in their place' take a toll on the lowlier baboons in the troop. They show the physiological signs of chronic stress and suffer more stress-related diseases. [6,7]

Psychological and social stressors

People also live in strict social hierarchies with patterns of dominance and subordination, and nowhere is this more apparent than in the workplace. If we wanted to design a way of working together which would be harmful to people we could not do worse than the way our large organisations have been set up. Since small organisations usually take the larger ones as their models they tend to have the same, negative effects on the people in them. The workplace has become the modern equivalent of the Cro-Magnon savannah – the place where our ancestors had to struggle for survival – as the environment where we are most likely to have to call on our atavistic survival responses. We may never have to outrun a sabre-toothed tiger on our way to the canteen, but parallel situations arise which have the same effect on our systems.

Because of the way organisations are structured, factors which affect stress in the workplace include inability to control the workload, little choice about how or when we work, depersonalisation, low sense of personal achievement, inconsistent or inconsiderate management styles, bad planning and a whole host of other factors often outside our control (or which we think are, which can have the same effect). On top of that there are more specific work-related stressors, such as the threat of redundancy, unfair treatment or the constant restructuring that has become a feature of the organisational landscape these days.

The psychosocial pressures that can lead to lower standards of physical and mental health (and consequently, higher death rates) are now well documented,[8] if not yet fully understood. Studies of Whitehall civil servants have shown that death from heart disease was four times higher among the most junior grades compared with the most senior. The author of the research says that the chronic stress associated with low job control in the work environment played a central role.[9, 10]

Many other studies have shown the detrimental effects of chronic stress caused by the pressure of demanding relationships. One group of researchers led by Janice Kiecolt-Glaser of Ohio State University[11] looked at the effects of chronic stress on long-term carers of people with Alzheimer's disease. The carer may face almost intolerable physical and emotional demands for many years as the sufferer becomes increasingly dependent and – since Alzheimer's affects brain function – alien to the carer, which all take their toll. Keicolt-

Glaser's research found that, in full-time caregivers, marked impairment of the immune system leaves them prey to a higher rate of physical illness, psychological distress and depression. There is also evidence that these effects do not disappear when the relationship ends. In a related study 43 per cent of the carers surveyed suffered from depression while their spouse was alive.[12] When these results were followed up three times over a period following the death of their partner, 41 per cent of respondents were still found to be suffering from mild to severe depression up to three years later. Rates of depression among a comparable group of non-carers was only 15 per cent. The negative effects of chronic stress can linger for years.

This might represent an extreme case. Caring for someone you love as you watch them withdraw into the world of dementia must bring its own horrors, quite apart from the stressful daily demands of caring. In fact, in the second group carers' stress did diminish on the death of the spouse, as one would expect, but significantly their psychological health did not improve.

Chronic stress has many damaging effects and health can continue to suffer long after the 'stressor' has ceased to be an active factor. In a healthy person the stress response is temporary and they return to normal quickly. When subjected to prolonged stress, however, they may lose this ability, irreversible changes take place, and their health can deteriorate further. [13]

What is significant about this when dealing with difficult people is that much of their behaviour may in fact be the side-effect of stress.

How stress affects our thinking

Stress does not just affect us physically, it also affects our thinking styles. If we remember that the stress response is a survival mechanism, it is easy to see why nature should have provided us with a means of reliably taking control when we are threatened. For example, consider today's sophisticated airliners with their computer-managed autopilot systems. During routine periods of operation, the system handles all the standard functions controlling speed, direction and altitude, actually flying the aircraft for long periods. The pilot is happy to sit back in a supervisory role as the plane flies itself through the clear blue sky. However, as more demanding situations arise – deteriorating weather conditions or an approach to landing, for example – the pilot takes a more 'hands on' responsibility for flying the plane. He or she may hesitate before doing this, sitting up, taking notice and attentively scanning the instruments to verify that human intervention is really needed before switching from automatic to manual control. Eventually complete control for the safety of the aircraft passes to the pilot.

Now consider this in relation to people. As we go about our routine business we are happy to coast along, more or less supervising our thought processes (on autopilot). Taxing situations at first make us more alert and we start contemplating our actions – our thinking actually gets sharper. But as an event becomes more threatening, nature (the pilot) quickly intervenes, wresting the controls from us, launching a pre-programmed mental survival routine designed to keep us safe. In the same way that the computer system is not considered sophisticated enough (yet) to allow it total control of the aircraft at certain times, so nature does not trust our judgement and thinking styles to be reliable or quick enough to safely run things when we are facing danger (a perceived threat). Remember that this survival response is a primitive one provided for life-and-death situations. It does not need to reason, only ensure that we come through a crisis with the best chance of staying alive. In the same way that our physical processes at such times are adapted to ensure only the essential functions needed to meet the challenge, so our cognitive processes, our thinking, is reduced to operating with the minimum of conscious intervention. A number of things happen which can distort our thinking and so how we view and interpret things.

Our thinking becomes polarised

All-or-nothing thinking forces us to make decisions quickly. It does not recognise shades of grey – things are either OK or they are not, good or bad, yes or no. We tend to jump to conclusions. Nature does not want us to reason when we are under threat. When faced with a complex challenge, we are primed to act quickly and practically in order to deal with it. [14, 15]

Concentration suffers

People under stress will often say that they feel confused, have difficulty concentrating or feel 'woolly' or muddled when trying to focus on anything that needs concentration. But thinking about the reason that we have a fight-or-flight response makes it obvious why this is: when facing a likely attack we do not need to reason, just act. When our primitive ancestors were trying to outrun tigers or fight off other predators, thinking about which defensive strategy to use, or reflecting on the deep meaning to be drawn from homo sapiens' perpetual struggle against the forces of nature, were activities to be discouraged. If I am about to be attacked by an enemy, nature wants me to act without considering mediation. Sure, some of us are spurred into action at the last minute – many people use the pressure of a looming deadline to write a report or prepare for an exam. But being subjected to longer-term or greater levels of stress reduces our ability to think straight. [16]

Memory is affected

Memory is also initially enhanced by mild stress. Most people have crystal clear recollections of their wedding day or the birth of their first child and, as the saying goes, everyone remembers where they were when they got the news of the attack on the World Trade Centre in New York. But we can also think of times when our memory totally failed us under pressure: an inability to recall a vital date or chemical formula during an exam, for example. Contestants on the TV game show *Who Wants to be a Millionaire* regularly say that it is far harder finding the right answers under the glare of the studio lights with an audience of millions than it ever was at home. And stress can do more lasting damage – it can be highly disruptive to memory[17]. The prolonged presence of stress hormones can cause long-term memory and recall to suffer, and in extreme cases memory loss can become permanent.[18]

We become hyperalert to threat

Joseph LeDoux says: 'Stress shifts us into a mode of operation where we react to danger rather than think about it.' It makes sense that a constellation of responses designed to keep us safe would include a tendency to spot threat early and take the necessary steps to protect ourselves. The result is that we often become defensive or feel constantly on edge as if 'something is about to happen'. We adopt conditioned responses as a reaction to threat.[19] In the office or while out shopping these responses may not be entirely appropriate.

Our mood changes

Stress can seriously affect our mood. Anger, irritability, anxiety and worry are some of the consequences of even mild stress. This in turn skews how we view things. Mood affects the judgements we make (and even how we make them).[20] Low or sad moods tend to make us view things more negatively than they really are,[21] and when we are angry our judgements and reactions tend to follow suit. As biopsychologist Robert Thayer says: 'In the final analysis, it is our reactions to life events, not the events themselves, that count the most. And these reactions are filtered through our prevailing moods.'[22] What is more, an excess of stress can lead to symptoms that are harder to shift, such as constant depression, phobias and even post-traumatic stress disorder (PTSD).[23]

Emotion and arousal

The reason I have taken so long outlining what happens to people under stress is that I believe that a lot of the difficult behaviour we have to contend with – our own and other people's – is due to the pressure we are under. I am not saying that we should therefore excuse bad behaviour on this basis. I am saying that greater awareness of the effects of stress makes it easier for us to de-personalise the behaviour when we see it in others. It also helps us to recognise that contributory factors in the modern workplace make people vulnerable to the negative effects of stress, which in turn predisposes us all to difficult or dysfunctional behaviour. Some people handle the stressors better than others, as we know. Indeed, the way each of us handles it will vary from day to day because our mood affects our judgement, on which we base our responses.

While there is no defence for bad behaviour in the workplace (or anywhere else for that matter), as a rule we tend to make allowances for people when we know they are having a hard time. Framing difficult behaviour as a product of circumstances the difficult person finds stressful, while not excusing them, does something to mitigate our beliefs about them.[24] It also gives a clue in how to deal with them because if their behaviour is due to stress, putting extra pressure on them is unlikely to be helpful.

First deal with the emotion

Have you ever been upset and tried to communicate how you feel to another person only to find that, far from acknowledging your distress, they try to put their side of the story? Or maybe you had a bad experience and just wanted someone to listen to you, but they responded by telling you their own troubles? Not very satisfactory, is it. What we want most when we are upset (or dis-stressed) is some sign from the other person that they recognise where we are coming from. We want someone to understand how we feel.

The old adage 'First deal with the emotion' is a useful reminder that, when dealing with a difficult person or for that matter anyone who appears troubled, we first need to acknowledge their view of the world. This can be done simply by listening (see Chapter 7), and by actively giving the impression both verbally (for example, 'How unfair!', 'That must have hurt', 'If I was in your position I'd be really mad'), and non-verbally (facial expressions, a touch, attentive posture) that we understand. Of course, such responses will only help if they are sincere: there is an absolute ban on phrases like 'I hear where you are coming from' or 'I really know how you feel, but...'.

In sickness and in health

Not all emotional arousal expresses itself as a display of anger. People under stress may respond in a variety of ways and, since stress in itself is not toxic (although chronic stress can produce toxic effects), not everyone becomes a difficult person. Having said that, many of the reactions in people whose behaviour we find difficult are due to the very same factors which are stressful to us all: doubt, uncertainty, threat of change, loss of status, fear of failing, lack of respect and so on. This list could go on and on and would of course include not just real-life events but also the individual's perceptions. If I *believe* you don't respect me or if I am *worried* about failing, the effects on my physiology can be the same as if the events were actually happening. For me they are real because I believe them.

And then there are life events that are more persistent. For example, extreme poverty is a considerable stressor in many people's lives. I am definitely not equating poverty with difficult behaviour but if I can't pay the rent or am worried about providing for the needs of my family, the pressure is bound to take its toll. Studies have clearly shown that social structure and social position (or rather, their relative inequalities in many societies) generate anxiety and stress.[25] Sickness, chronic pain and loneliness are just a few of the other circumstances likely to provoke difficult behaviour and which we may fail to consider when confronted with say, a Steamroller (see page 127) or a Grouser (see page 173).

Communication and confusion

Virginia Satir, the American psychologist who pioneered much innovative work in the field of family therapy, identified four patterns of behaviour that people unknowingly adopt as a reaction to the negative effects of stress. These four patterns are the ways in which we respond when we feel that our self-esteem is under threat or in some way diminished.[26]

Satir says: *'When one is doubtful about one's worth it is easy to use another's actions and reactions to define oneself... I recommend you treat everything that comes to you from the outside as something with which to cope, not as a way of defining yourself.'* And so in relation to stressful events: *'Likewise, stress alone need not feel like an attack on self-worth. Feeling stress might be painful or annoying, but it isn't the same as doubting your own worth.'*[27]

Think for a moment about somebody you have known whom you would classify as a difficult person. Then think about what Satir is proposing here, namely, that when a person feels unsure of their ground in some way this can provoke a negative reaction in them. To put it another way, how often could you say – at the times you have encountered difficult behaviour (or have become difficult yourself) – that the person being difficult felt truly safe, confident and in control?[28]

Remembering that the stress response is about survival, and that the 'threat' can be real or perceived, any time I feel that my self-esteem is at risk I am likely to react in an emotionally driven, rather than a reasoned and prepared way. This causes trouble because, quite apart from what is going on inside me, my communications will be confusing and often misunderstood by those I interact with.

Noticing over many years the conditioned stances people

typically use as a defence mechanism in reaction to threat, Satir says that people:

Blame – so they appear strong.

Placate – so that others don't get angry.

Compute – in order to neutralise the threat.

Distract – to draw attention away from the threat.

The Blamer is a fault-finder, a dictator, a boss who acts in a superior way that seems to be saying, 'Why am I the only one around here who gets things done?' When we are in Blaming mode we are only interested in giving orders, criticising and finding fault to hide the fact that we really don't feel that we count for much. The Blamer appears, shouting and gesticulating, when inside we feel isolated or fear failure.

The Placater is submissive and deferential: always aiming to please, apologising and agreeing, no matter what. The Placater always needs someone else's approval. If you want to know how a Placater feels, it helps to think of yourself as unimportant... you owe everybody gratitude which you not only say but show by your ingratiating behaviour. Inside you feel worthless and needy.

The behaviour of a Computer is always correct, totally reasonable, with no show of feeling. The person seems calm, cool and collected. They could be compared to an actual computer or a dictionary. Their self-worth hides behind big words and intellectual concepts. There is no 'life' in the body at all, everything is happening in the head. They cover their sense of vulnerability by becoming technical, analytical or moving into the abstract.

The Distracter is a master of the irrelevant. That is, irrelevant to the question in hand. This person cannot answer directly or to the point. They often appear dizzy, distracted, as if their mind is all over the place. When in Distracter mode people can be affable and amiable, but with a gift for non sequiturs and detours. It is as though ignoring the threat will make it go away: the feeling is that 'nobody cares, I don't really belong here'.

Behaviours, not characters

Once we have identified any of these behaviours it is very easy to make the next small, and mistaken, step to believing that these are labels with which to identify people. They most definitely are not. Blamers or Placaters are not 'characters' any of us might meet, rather they describe behaviours that people drop into at certain times when under stress. Recognising that someone is in Computer or Distracter mode is to identify how they are acting at that moment, rather than to label them pejoratively. One way of considering these behaviours is as products of the relationship in which they occur. They arise only in the context of human interaction, in response to another person.

We all do some of these things at different times. When faced with a situation that makes us feel unsure or unsafe we are likely to default to one of the above modes of behaviour. For example, these four stances underlie most human negotiations when there is any sort of tension or pressure.[29] Understanding and recognising them is therefore a key factor in the process of dealing with difficult people.

The final, and crucial, point here is what is known as incongruence – the outward behaviour that people adopt in the face of a 'threat' does not match what they are feeling inside. This makes it difficult to read their actions in an attempt to plan our response.

The whole message

'It is important to understand that every time you talk, all of you talks', says Satir. Our communications are made up of the words we say, of course, but the importance of the non-verbal parts of the message is often overlooked. Facial expressions, muscle tone, gestures, posture, breathing, as well as different facets of speech such as volume, tempo, rhythm, pitch, tonality and inflection all play their part.[30] Our exchanges are judged on all of these aspects and any discrepancy between verbal and non-verbal parts results in a double-message: words are saying one thing and all the other parts are saying something else. Most of us will have had the disappointing experience of hearing someone say those magic words, 'I love you', and not believing them. With any luck, and hopefully since that time, we have also had the same words said to us in a way that we did believe – same words, different message (and usually different people). For more on this see Chapter 7, *Listening and rapport: neglected skills.*

We can all think of times when our behaviour has fallen neatly into one of the descriptions above (if we can't see it in ourselves, our family or colleagues can), and when our feelings of uncertainty, fear, doubt or whatever led us to adopt a stance we had not initially intended or which surprised us. Perhaps you entered a discussion cool, calm and collected, only to find that five minutes later you had totally 'lost it', despite your best intentions (Blamer); or you have changed the subject unintentionally or told an inappropriate joke in the middle of an important discussion (Distracter); or maybe you had gone to ask your boss for a rise and had every intention of being polite yet definitely assertive, but five minutes later you had fallen into a version of 'yes-sir-no-sir-three-bags-full-sir'. Apologising for your existence and for wasting everyone's time, you left without getting what you wanted (Placater).

This is not to say that we should not blame, distract, placate or compute if it is appropriate to do so. Has someone done something wrong which caused upset or inconvenience and you think blame would be useful? Go ahead. You find yourself in the unfortunate position of having someone in front of you waving an axe and they're not chopping firewood? For God's sake, placate them (or better still, run).

Adopting any of these stances by choice – rather than unconsciously – is not harmful in the way Satir describes because our words and actions will be a true reflection of our thoughts and feelings. The vital difference is that we know what we are doing and understand the consequences. In other words we take responsibility for our behaviour without trying to pretend it isn't happening or pointing the finger at another person.

Levelling

You might wonder, if we are all so good at sending out confusing messages, how we manage at all. One of the keys to successful communications is that all parts of the message agree – words match the facial expression, body language, voice volume and tone. This response, known as levelling, relieves the need to retreat into any of the dysfunctional modes above. When levelling, we tell it like it is, our messages are congruent. When the leveller says: 'Good to see you', the words are delivered with warmth and sincerity, the face is open and welcoming. If the words are 'I am really mad with you', this will also be reflected in the angry tone of voice and tightness in the body language.

This directness and congruence contrast to a placating response, for example, where the speaker is feeling fear or apprehension but acting in a conciliatory way, or a computing response where he or she feels vulnerable but is covering it by retreating into the abstract or the technical and showing no emotion.

Because the levelling response is whole, the message is not split or concealed, it is openly delivered in an honest way. The added advantage is that in order to do this we first have to know what we are thinking and feeling (two different things) and what we want to say. This in itself tends to lead to a more levelling kind of approach because it helps us to be objective about our own behaviour. When dealing with a difficult person who may be shouting at us (blaming) it will not help if we start up in the same mode. Neither would I recommend that you start to analyse their behaviour by explaining that they are only in blaming mode because they really feel worthless or insignificant. So, when faced with a bombastic 'What's the matter with you, don't you hear anything I say?', rather than shrieking back: 'Me not hearing? That's rich, you never listen to a word I say!', try instead: 'Did I miss something? Sorry, could you tell me again?'

Some years ago a woman at one of my seminars said: 'If I did this levelling business in most of my relationships pretty soon I wouldn't have any relationships left.' Sure, it can seem unreasonable to go round telling the plain, unvarnished truth the whole time. In fact, people who do that are judged as lacking the vital skill of empathy. The real message here is that if our communications are not working, or if our relationship with a difficult person needs help, we should make sure that we are truly expressing what we want to say about how we think and feel. And there is no reason to be blunt or hurtful in saying something like 'I'd like to talk to you but I'm worried about how you might react', rather than 'Fine' when it is not.

Gender-specific responses

A subject guaranteed to start a debate at the dinner table is that men and women see the world differently. We are all agreed that we differ biologically – that the structure and functions of our bodies prepare us for different things – but the idea that male and female thinking styles are also different can cause heated debate. Push the matter further by saying that these differences are due to the psychological attributes of the sexes (nature), rather than socialisation (nurture), and you'll really turn up the heat and arouse passions.

This is a vast and intriguing topic that has already generated a number of successful books and even a stage show or two. These have struck a popular chord, which suggests that we all intuitively know that the temperament and behaviour of the sexes are quite different, even if the public policy documentation generally ignores it.[31] This is not the place to explore the subject fully, my reason in mentioning it at all in relation to dealing with difficult people is that gender-specific responses, both psychological and physiological, can and do lead to misunderstandings and friction. This comes as no surprise to most of us, but to date many of the attempts to produce greater harmony between the sexes have been aimed at reconciling these differences rather than recognising and celebrating them.

Neither better nor worse

Perhaps it is a legacy from our recent history where social attitudes and expectations have placed such a burden on both the sexes to change that has led to this discussion frequently becoming an argument. The point is not whether men or women are better or worse, right or wrong, nor is it about comparisons or justifications. It is about explanation and understanding. The more we understand about our typical responses and those of the other sex the less excuse we have for misinterpreting them.

Deborah Tannen, the professor of linguistics whose book *You Just Don't Understand* brought her worldwide recognition, says: 'Pretending that women and men are the same hurts women because the ways they are treated are based on the norms for men. It also hurts men who, with good intentions, speak to women as though they would to men, and are nonplussed when their words don't work as expected, and even spark resentment and anger.'[32]

Another author, psychologist Elizabeth Mapstone, sets out to show that: 'Relationships are central to how people interpret disagreements with each other. Not only does it matter how well you know the other person, how intimate you are, whether you like or dislike him or her, or which of you has the higher status: gender turns out to be one of the most important factors of all.'[33]

Stress and gender

Since we all accept that the biology of a man's body is different from that of a woman's, from there it is a small step to acknowledge that the nervous and endocrine systems that control our physical and emotional responses (including the stress response) by definition must operate differently too, and that this leads to divergent emotional styles.[34]

For example, in face-to-face conflict a man's heartbeat will rise more quickly, go higher and stay up longer than a woman's. Remember that heartbeat, emotional arousal and the effects of the fight-or-flight response are all interlinked. Men are not as effective at self-calming as women and, should the conflict persist (or something a man reads as conflict), will generally shut down or withdraw from the conversation sooner than a woman would.

Before you go running away with the idea that this just proves how men can't handle their emotions, let's consider the other half of the equation. Women, for their part, are more inclined than men to raise sensitive issues, but are more likely to do so head-on using what John Gottman calls a 'harsh start-up'. Females can also handle greater emotional 'heat' without becoming dysfunctional (from a woman's point of view that is – men often view displays of emotions by a woman as highly dysfunctional or at least emotional and illogical).[35] Therein lies the problem, at least in the domestic setting. It is characteristic of heterosexual relationships that when conflict occurs the female is more comfortable with, and even expects, a certain level of emotional arousal. The male, by contrast, being less comfortable with raised emotional arousal, tends to read it as a danger signal and shuts down (stonewalls).[36]

Consider how this is a recipe for disaster. The sexes experience their particular levels of emotional response differently. Picture the scene: the more she demands, the further he withdraws. It would be comical if it were not for the different interpretations we put on these two behaviours.

While the man is thinking: 'This is not worth a fight, if I keep quiet things will calm down and then we can discuss it', the woman is interpreting his withdrawal as a sign of his refusal to discuss the issue. She equates emotion with the urgency of the situation, he sees it as a threat. What is more, these individualised ways of responding are not something our bodies have much choice about. We are made that way. Typically, this means that as a woman steps up her demands to talk, the man will withdraw behind the newspaper (or into the computer screen). Evidently, these are stereotypical responses and I am not intending in these simplified examples to label men or women as helpless automatons or slaves to their gender. The patterns of behaviour, nevertheless, hold true sufficiently often for most people to be able to identify with them to some extent.

He said, she said

Tannen speaks about what she calls 'rapport talk' and 'report talk' to explain one aspect of how men and women use language differently. Women see conversation as a means of building rapport, while men use it in an attempt to maintain status. What this means in the real world, especially the world of work, is that men tend to rationalise their way out of disagreements with women by being 'right' and using, as they see it, faultless logic. Their style of speaking and listening also tends (by consequence rather than intent) to minimise or discount women's contributions. Banter, put-downs and mock challenges help them avoid feeling one-down in the situation. Women, on the other hand, though they are just as capable of using the same strategies as men, do not do so intuitively. They tend to work more to maintain an appearance of equality, encourage consensus, downplay hierarchical difference.[37] They are better at diplomacy and reading the other person's non-verbal language. On the downside they can often misinterpret men's banter and posturing as a put-down or bloody-mindedness. Elizabeth Mapstone found in her studies that arguments between opposite sex colleagues resulted in differing views:

• In disputes with female colleagues three-quarters of men thought the women did not hear what they had said, but two-thirds of women's reports said the men did hear.

• Men judged the arguments as 'not important' while women saw them as 'very important'.

These findings[38] and others point to the view that the sexes can experience the same incident differently because of their different communication styles and the criteria by which they judge the importance of an interaction and its outcome: status, winning and losing, or consensus, discussion and understanding. This incompatibility may lead to difficulties in relationships under normal circumstances, and exacerbate the difficulties under stressful conditions.[39]

Women are more sensitive to relationship issues, communicate more equitably, and respond to distress in ways that are more emotional and less aggressive or assertive. Men, on the other hand, focus less on relationships, tend to be more aggressive and assertive, and respond to stress with more instrumental and problem-solving behaviours.[40] These divergent styles – arising out of our different biological responses to stress – have been termed 'tend and befriend' versus 'fight and flight.' Females are more likely to respond to stress by nurturing their relationships and reaching out to others, whereas men are more likely to withdraw into themselves or initiate confrontation.[41]

Divided by a common language

Men deal with the raised emotion by diminishing its importance – they see it as incidental to the interaction – whereas women recognise emotional arousal as a sign that contact has been made, as a fundamental part of the interaction. Once again, this highlights the fact that the sexes are, to paraphrase George Bernard Shaw, 'divided by a common language'.

In this brief summary I have not done justice to the huge amount of research that has been conducted by psychologists over the last two decades into the particularities and patterns of gender communication.

The key points I want to get across are that there really is a strong case for understanding the language of the sexes which Deborah Tannen calls 'genderlect'. This places us in different cultures and, like any cultural differences, two-way respect is as important as understanding the language. If we cannot understand the language of the other culture at least we can know it exists.

The second point I would like to clarify is that I have not intended in any way to say that one is better than the other. We accept that men have, in general, more facial hair than women and that women, in general, are physically a little smaller than men. We must also accept that other differences exist without the matter turning into some sort of contest.

With regard to comments like 'not all men/women are like that...' that this sort of discussion usually provokes, of course they are not. These gender differences are tendencies and should not be taken as rigid or applying to all members of the sex in question. Garth Fletcher, Director of the International Society for the Study of Personal Relationships, says: 'Differences within genders in relationships are almost always much greater than the differences between genders.'[42] For any of the 'typical' gender responses there will be a significant proportion of that sex who are exceptions to the rule. While women (generally) tend to favour consensus, discussion and understanding in their communications there are, of course, many men who do too. In the same way there are plenty of women for whom status and winning or losing are powerful motivations in their lives.

What to do about it

I am working on the basis that any ideas that contribute to handling difficult behaviour more productively will be welcome. I am not going to offer gender-specific strategies because I do not think that there are any beyond the general advice offered elsewhere in this book. Nevertheless, by way of summary some pointers will, I hope, be useful:

- Miscommunications happen for the most unlikely reasons. Check out possible misinterpretations, on both sides.

- Resist the temptation to follow your assumptions; give the other person the benefit of the doubt. If the problem persists, ask yourself: 'What might I have missed?'

- Check that it really is a problem for you both. You may be more aware of it than they are, or reading the wrong part of the message. Ask about it.

- Seek first to understand the other person – aim to listen non-defensively (see Chapter 10).

- Assume best intent. Take the position that they mean well, that you simply have confusion due to a culture or language gap.

- Separate impact from intent, the effect on you may not be the effect they intended (see Chapter 10).

- Respect that 'different' does not mean 'deficient'. There are many truths and trying to impose ours on another will just make us difficult too.

I have just touched on some of the differences that can lead to confused communications. We need to see our understanding as lacking rather than the other person as deficient. Above all, we need to see the emotional response (or lack of it) as a part of the communication rather than interpreting it as over-excitement (or under-involvement).

Much of what we refer to as difficult behaviour is simply the by-product of being human, but being human also means the ability in most of us to mediate our emotional responses. In other words, even though under the 'right' circumstances we can all become difficult (indeed we are designed to be), we can exercise control over those responses that might upset or alienate other people and gum up the workings of our relationships with them.

Empathy and direct communication

Self-awareness, the ability to reflect on our thoughts and behaviour, is linked to our ability to empathise with and understand others. Indeed, our working model for understanding others is ourselves. The downside is that people will tend to attribute to others their own motives and designs. Just as we need to be aware of our own assumptions we also need to understand the limitations of applying them uncritically to others.

In this chapter, the last one in this section, I have outlined what I think is one of the most important aspects to what we frequently term 'difficult behaviour'. Much of the conduct we find difficult to handle in others is simply people behaving as people do when they feel pressured, threatened, uncertain or fearful. Of course, many would not recognise this or agree with the idea that they felt, say, vulnerable or uncertain. If they did they would probably handle their stress in some way other than becoming difficult. And I am certainly not suggesting that we should respond to difficult behaviour by openly acknowledging their emotion or enquiring about their feelings at every turn.[43] Good communicators, however, have good empathy skills. This means that they are able to pick up on and respond appropriately to the other person's emotional state.

Another common factor in disputes are the misunderstandings about differences in gender psychology that can exacerbate interpersonal conflict. Once again, I am not saying that these differences cause the problems. But the gender-based stances and responses we typically use – through misinterpretation or preconceptions which attach themselves to members of both sexes – can render the already tricky terrain of human communications even more confusing.

Finally, the strategies outlined in the next section give more 'bullet-pointed' ideas on the subject of the book. In thinking about how and when to apply them it is vitally important to know the emotional state of the person we are dealing with, because it is hard, if not impossible, to get the attention or change the behaviour of someone who is distressed.

SECTION 2

Chapter 6
The seven key skills

In naming this chapter I have used the term 'key skills', though it is really more accurate to refer to 'groups of skills' or 'key stages', since the points refer to a number of steps which should be carried out or at least seriously considered before taking any action on difficult behaviour. However, I have been referring to these as skills for a number of years now and the term is useful because it focuses us on three essential aspects of the process that this book is intended to help:

- As I have already mentioned, the aim of the exercise is not to put down, point-score or 'win'. Any such stance is doomed to failure in the long term because it is likely to prolong or amplify the differences between ourselves and the difficult person and simply increase the tension. It also weakens our own position. The focus should be on *our* attitudes and skills, and the actions we take to bring about the result we want.

- Point two is that in order to implement any course of action or exercise choice over our actions, we need to be in control of our thoughts and feelings, rather than them running us, ie develop self-management skills.

- And the third point? Clearly, if you have identified a person or a situation that you often encounter as difficult and you are reading this, you have not yet resolved things in the way you'd like. My rule when something isn't working is to try a different tack. And this will mean thinking or acting differently, or both. Forward planning is essential and the points below act as a checklist of the skills needed to go about it.

1. Preparation – know your aim

In order to arrive at our destination (our desired result), first we need to know where we want to go or what it is we want to achieve. Someone once said: 'If you don't know where you are going, you will wind up somewhere else.'[1] Have you ever started a conversation with a difficult person without knowing the outcome you want? Most of us have. In fact, the greater the difficulty we are having with another person, the more likely we are to stumble on without a clear idea of where we are going. We may know very well we want a solution, but are not sure of how to get there.

However, we must have a goal, only then can we start moving towards it. A useful step at this point is to ask ourselves questions like, 'How do I want this to end?', 'What would I like to happen as a result of this discussion?' and 'In an ideal world, if the problem didn't exist any more, what would I be doing differently?'

The preparation under this heading also means thinking about our strategy, as well as planning how, when and where we are going to implement it. This is an essential step in any project. It should identify whether we have the resources to carry our plan through and, equally, any that might be lacking.

For example, it is one thing to decide that the next time your boss picks on you to work late you'll politely reply with an assertive 'Thanks for choosing me but I am unable to do any more overtime this month', but it is quite another thing to do it. You may need to prepare by practising the words, developing some assertiveness skills or coping with your own emotions, such as anxiety or guilt.

If you regularly have to deal with members of the public who shout or threaten you, reading the suggested strategies for dealing with the Steamroller will help you plan, but you may also need to practise. If, in the face of somebody else's tirade you have never responded with a cool 'Mrs Robinson, you interrupted me', then rehearsing the words (and also the situation if you can arrange for someone less threatening to shout at you) will increase your chances of handling the attack with more composure. For the best chance of getting the result we want, it is crucial to prepare our approach, plan our strategy and rehearse our lines.

2. Setting boundaries and limits

Even the best-laid plans can fail, indeed they often do, because the other person 'wrong foots' us by changing tack or saying something we had not expected. Even when we know exactly what we want to achieve and have decided on how to go about it, the other person can still catch us out and we find our resolve slipping. It is important to know our boundaries and limits because these will guide us. It is also important that the other person knows we have limits and that we are capable of reminding them where we stand.

To use the angry member of the public example again, I am often surprised by the number of people I meet who – though they are very unhappy at being shouted at in the course of their work – do nothing about it. If a total stranger walked into the reception area where you work and started to treat you with disrespect, how would you respond? Some people tell me that they can accept shouting but not personal insults, others that they can cope with insults but not swearing, while others say that they can recognise that the attack was aimed at the system and not them, so they don't take it personally. Some people will not discuss things while being shouted at, others will accept quite a lot before calling a halt and still others will soldier on valiantly in the belief that they do not have the right to defend themselves. There are dozens of other possible responses. None of these reactions is the 'right' one but each suggests a different set of boundaries.

Setting boundaries is a matter of personal choice, but to get another person's respect each of us first has to know where our boundaries are. This does not mean that we have to be rigid about them; they may change according to circumstances. For example, staff who work with client groups likely to be distressed by virtue of their circumstances are generally more tolerant of difficult behaviour in a work setting than if it occurred elsewhere.

If boundaries are, by definition, subject to a degree of flexibility then we need limits to set the point at which we call a halt. When, having prepared our strategy and tackled the difficult situation to the best of our abilities, we are still coming up against behaviour that exceeds our capacity to remain resourceful and feel in control, we need a cut-off point. Again, this may be linked to context because in some situations at work we may be prevented from walking away by our professional code of conduct or responsibilities. Most employers these days have clear protocols for protecting staff in the face of extreme behaviour, but there is often a mismatch between what people think they are allowed to do and what their instincts tell them to do.[2] Ideally, when dealing with difficult behaviour at work, both employer and employee should have agreed and understood acceptable limits. I often find, however, that this apparently simple statement provokes a lot of illuminating debate when I am leading workshops in organisations.

3. Staying cool, remaining objective

'If you can keep your head when all about you are losing theirs...' – Kipling's poem reminds us of the route to take when faced with the often unreasonable demands of the world around us.

Unfortunately, his perceptive poetic contribution was entitled *If* and not *How*. We all know the wisdom of remaining cool, calm and collected but at the moments when we need it most the skill seems to abandon us. Emotional arousal is the enemy of objectivity, so to remain in control and resourceful we need (a) sufficient emotional awareness to recognise when we are getting irritated or angry; and (b) the self-management skills to remain calm and therefore hang on to our objectivity. We also need to recognise when we have gone past our own personal point of no return, so that we can call a halt or at least get a breathing space and regain some sense of control if necessary. The secret here is to give ourselves choices. Emotions such as anger, anxiety or fear do precisely the opposite – they limit our choices.

Emotions have evolved to help us survive, to push us into behaviour aimed at getting a result (keeping safe, for example), so emotional arousal tends to limit our range of options. Daniel Goleman, in his bestseller *Emotional Intelligence*, very aptly calls this process 'emotional hijacking'. The phrase perfectly captures the way we can be taken over by our emotions. The same process convinces us that we have a greater degree of control than is in fact the case; when adrenalin is running the show we are not.

Step one is understanding when we may be at risk. We need to recognise when our feelings are starting to take over before we become the victim of an emotional hijacking. Step two is knowing what to do if we do start to get angry or fearful (or otherwise aroused) when dealing with someone we find difficult. In other words, we need to know how to calm ourselves down.

One of the things I have noticed in countless conversations I have had about this over the years, is that many people do not recognise their own indicators of emotional arousal early enough to do something about it. When I ask them how they know that they are starting to get upset with another person, they mention symptoms like confused thinking, sweating, tight breathing, raised pulse, butterflies in the stomach and so on. I respond by asking, if these are the early-warning signs, then what are the early-early-warning signs? In other words, how can they spot sooner that they might be at risk? Most of the indicators mentioned above are not early warning signs at all, they indicate that the emotional response is well under way. There are some hints on remaining calm in a later section (see the ASSUME technique on page 183). The main point is that we need to retain the ability to think objectively when handling difficult people.

Although a highly charged emotional response can sometimes be used deliberately to get a point across, I do not recommend it as a strategy. Because of the seductive nature of our emotions, it is all too easy to slip from mock anger into the real thing. Emotional outbursts also stop other people taking us seriously, particularly in the case of women. As psychologist Elizabeth Mapstone found in her research in the workplace: 'Most women have probably been told at some time that they are "over reacting".'[3] This is more likely when the person they are interacting with is a man, but both sexes tend to judge a person in terms of their emotions rather than assessing the argument. This, says David Fontana, is 'the kiss of death to any sustained hopes of influencing decision-making.'[4]

4. First deal with the emotion

The ability to handle our own emotions gives us a useful insight into dealing with difficult people. There is a rule of thumb in communications where there is tension, and that is 'first deal with the emotion'. In practical terms this means calming someone down before trying to deal with the issues.

Emotions frequently become entangled with the objective merits of the problem. When dealing with outright confrontation, anger or hostility it is quite easy to see when someone's emotions may be complicating the debate. In other circumstances it may be less obvious. When people start to feel uncertain or out of their depth, the resulting worry or anxiety can powerfully influence their behaviour. Faced with a new work routine, role or responsibilities, some people can become difficult. The best route through this is to allay their fears or doubts before trying to move them on. All too often this factor is missed.

Just how we do this will depend on the situation and the individual. In some cases it may be sufficient to acknowledge the uncertainty with a phrase like: 'I know, this makes us all feel uncertain'. Other times more exploration of a person's ideas and beliefs about a situation may be necessary before proceeding. Some people may become even more difficult at the mere mention of 'emotions' so a more 'softly, softly' approach – building rapport to strengthen trust and confidence – might be recommended.

It helps to be able to imagine ourselves in the other person's place. Being able to empathise, that is, understand how the other person might be feeling or at least understanding that they do have feelings, is different from the potentially ruminative process of looking for cause (asking why). Other hints include watching for the less obvious signs of emotional arousal, for example, increased voice tension or volume, quickened breathing, flushed skin tone, sulks or refusal to continue the conversation. Always remember that others might need more information; we may well know more than they do about a given situation or be able to handle it better.

5. Speaking clearly

It may seem like an odd question, but how often do you speak without knowing what you want to say? I am not saying that we do not choose the words we use; most of the time we do and some people do it with great care and precision. However, the underlying principle is that the impact of our communication should match our intent. In good communication the speaker ensures that the message he or she sends accurately reflects what they want to say in such a way that the hearer can hear it 'correctly'. The message accurately portrays the speaker's thoughts, wishes and feelings.

Sadly, we all know how often this formula is not adhered to. We can unintentionally produce a mismatch between intention and impact for a variety of reasons. One of these is that the speaker's way of sending the message is not consistent with the intent. For example, someone in a bad mood may sound more harsh than they intend to. The mood may have nothing to do with the recipient of the message. The reverse may also be true; someone who is mad with a colleague may cover it up and not express their true feelings. The main problem is that we all 'filter' our words in ways we may not be aware of. The listener also filters, of course, so their mood, beliefs or expectations will colour what they 'hear'. The formula has so many flaws it is a wonder our communications succeed at all.

Speaking clearly means doing all we can to eliminate the possibility for misunderstanding. This can be helped if we know what we want to say, know the intention behind it and know the outcome we want. We can also listen attentively to the response we get to assess whether the message our listener says they received is the same as the message we thought we'd sent.

6. Listening to understand

Listening is an underrated art – it is the thread that holds all communications together. I am not just thinking about the auditory function of communications here, because 'listening' involves far more than using our ears. The actual process is covered in more detail in the next chapter. Good listening is a dynamic, two-way process. It involves hearing, checking understanding and demonstrating that the message has been heard. Alas, there are very few examples of good listening practice to be found in life's daily interactions.

Of course, some people are probably better listeners because it is a fundamental part of the job for which they have been trained. Nevertheless, the daily demonstrations we witness from those around us – particularly when we are young and therefore learning the habits we will carry through into adulthood – fail to teach us much about the true qualities of listening. Whether it is the high-profile interactions of politics and the media or more prosaic exchanges, there are very few instances of good practice. Needless to say, this is especially true when tensions are running high.

7. Knowing where to end

When dealing with a difficult person or situation, observing the points above will ensure a good start and in some cases will be all that is needed to clear up a misunderstanding or establish a more productive working relationship. Starting with these steps and developing your chosen strategy will pay dividends, but there is one more factor which I think has to be considered before starting, and it is this – how will you know when to end?

Sometimes all that is needed to put a stop to difficult behaviour is a quiet word at the right time and under the right circumstances. In other situations more concerted and persistent tactics might be required. Whatever the case, when planning our goal it is valuable to consider the point at which we will feel that we have achieved what we set out to do. Over the years I have repeatedly been told stories that challenge the pessimistic adage about old dogs and new tricks. If the difficult person is going to take your message on board then, provided that it is delivered with clarity, you will not need to go on about it once you have made your point. If they are not showing signs of understanding, are resisting you or becoming defensive, then equally, it is time to withdraw and rethink your ideas. Prolonged assault runs the risk of making things worse.

There is another reason for knowing when to end when dealing with a difficult person. If you have to get a Guerrilla to give up their habits, stop a Steamroller or educate an Expert, there is a lot to be said for brevity. Once the message has been delivered or the other recommended steps have been taken, you should avoid the temptation to extend the conversation unnecessarily. Keeping it brief will deprive them of the opportunity to use more of the behaviour you are trying to change. Leaving them to it will also give them a little time to reflect. Who knows, they might use the time wisely.

Chapter 7

Listening and rapport: neglected skills

Non-defensive listening

Listening effectively is a much-neglected skill, probably because it is far harder to do than is generally realised. In addition we are not generally shown, either in school or elsewhere, how to listen to what is going on around us. I maintain that improved listening in society as a whole could dramatically alter how we react to many of the social problems we are facing today, and consequently start to reduce them.

Some of us have been taught listening skills as part of our professional training, but even then we are given remarkably little indication by our teachers of how effective we actually are as listeners. It is assumed that because we have attended a certain amount of training we must have acquired the skills. I, for one, had not, and I have to work constantly at hearing what my clients, family and others say to me.

This is because listening is an interactive process and, like all other interpersonal skills, it needs constant practice to keep it in shape. Other factors have an impact on how we listen. The quality of the relationship between speaker and listener will affect not just what is said, but how it is said, how it is received and the filters that may be unwittingly applied on both sides. Factors such as anxiety, stress and fatigue also reduce our listening performance, as do our assumptions, judgements and personal 'agendas'. A more satisfactory model for listening involves hearing the speaker's words and feelings, attempting to grasp the meaning, then checking our understanding with them.

To listen effectively means adhering to four main principles:

- The first of these is to take a non-defensive stance. We can all think of times when we have been more concerned with putting our point across than we were to hear the other person's view. To really listen we have to put aside our own needs for a moment and pay full attention to the speaker.

- We must also focus on the factual content of the speaker's words, paying particular attention to what makes sense in what they are saying, rather than what is wrong with it. This is because a judgemental listening stance will hinder understanding - it tends to pinpoint blame rather than identify contribution.

- We should be aware of the non-verbal aspects of the conversation. Listening to factual information is only one part of the process and generally the easiest part. It is at this superficial level that many people get caught out. It is very easy to start mentally checking out what is said, comparing it with our own version of things, analysing the content and interpreting what the speaker means. Rather than getting too absorbed in this part of the process, it is helpful to read what we can of the speaker's behaviour and delivery for clues to their emotional state. Understanding that they have feelings also helps to keep us more objective, and letting them know we understand something of how they feel is a critical part or successful communication. This is because it validates their right to feel as they do and tends to reduce their need to step up their demands to be heard.

- Fourth, and linked to the last point, the listener must demonstrate that they have heard and understood the speaker. An effective listener will be giving the speaker their full attention, demonstrating this non-verbally with open and receptive body language, appropriate eye contact, nods and other responses to back up the verbal 'nods' (uh-huh, I see, and so on) that we all use to show we are paying attention. In addition, summarising your understanding of the speaker's words *as well as their sentiments* are the hallmarks of effective listening. A simple remark such as 'That must be irritating' or 'In your position I'd be hopping mad' will let them know you have understood something of their position.

Checklist: non-defensive listening

1. Give the speaker your full attention, roughly matching (or mirroring) their body language – for more details see rapport building below.

2. Listen attentively, only asking questions to increase your understanding of their words and feelings. Remember: first seek to understand.

3. Summarise regularly. Feed back what you have heard (paraphrase, not parrot) as briefly as you can and include a comment from time to time which lets them know you have grasped how they feel about it, as well as what they think.

4. Ensure that your focus of attention is on them rather than on your own thought processes. Reading the 'whole person' will help you do this: notice things like their breathing, skin tone, body language, pupil dilation and so on. Listen, too, for signs of tension or strain in their voice, jumbled or unclear words and phrases, and repetitive comments that could give clues to their emotional state or a point they are struggling to make.

When listening, remember that we all tend to step up our attempts to be heard when we feel our audience is not understanding us (see Chapter 3). We might do this by getting louder or some other means of getting attention. If you notice someone becoming more difficult as you interact with them, this may be a sign that they are not getting the message that you are getting the message. Rather than assuming that they are a 'bad person' out to get you, try asking yourself 'What have I missed?', or 'What does this person need to hear from me to let them know that I have understood their message?'

Miller's Law

It might be useful to remember Miller's Law, which says:

> 'In order to understand what another person is saying, you must assume that it is true and try to find out what it could be true of.'[1]

In other words, accept what they say at face value as being true *for them*. This does not mean that you have to agree with their statement, but that you are suspending judgement pending further information. You're acting as if temporarily it is true (which it probably is for them). You then listen carefully to find out what their reasons are for thinking the statement is true, and what it is true *of*.

In general, people like to talk more than they like to listen, but it is the listener who controls the conversation. And, like any other skill, there is no substitute for practice.

Rapport building: harmony of interaction

When we are in agreement or harmony with someone else we tend to move into rapport with that person. Have you noticed, when walking with someone, how much better it feels if your stride and rhythm match theirs, and how odd it can feel when you are 'out of step'? Watch people who are interacting well together, say, in a restaurant or a pub. Two people standing or sitting and conversing will generally adopt mirror images of each other. Not only that, their facial expressions, voice tone and rhythm, even the language they use will begin to match (this is clearly visible among groups of children or teenagers, who will adopt the same language, accent and style of dress as their peers within days or even hours of arriving in a new class). The same kind of unconscious matching goes on anywhere where people are interacting well; there tends to be an automatic process of non-verbal communication as they attempt to achieve a sense of 'oneness' with each other. [2]

Rapport signals a relationship characterised by agreement, alignment, likeness or similarity. When we amplify what we share, resistance and antagonism are reduced and even disappear. People are automatically drawn to others that they see as being like themselves. It's a question of 'people liking people who have the good sense to like them'. [3]

In situations marked by conflict or differences of opinion – such as when handling a difficult person – rapport building makes it easier for us to ally ourselves with our adversary. It is a skill that can be practised easily when we are with other people, though it must be done with subtlety. The aim is to roughly match the other person's body position and gestures (taking care not to ape or mimic). If they are standing, stand, if they are sitting, sit. Aim for symmetry with them: if their arms are crossed adopt a roughly similar position with yours, if the person is propping up the doorframe, lean on the wall to echo their position.

With more practice, various aspects of speech patterns can also be matched. Go for the main characteristics. If the person speaks very slowly and you speak fast, slow down a little. If they are speaking loudly and you have a softer voice, raise yours (though not above theirs, which could make things worse). With a little practice this becomes natural - which it is, after all – a kind of dance of communication.

Practising these skills is easy because all it takes is to become consciously aware of something we all do anyway, and then to develop it for purposeful use in situations where it could help to build rapport deliberately. The best classroom for understanding this process is the real world, such as watching how people behave in bars and at work, or noticing the interactions on chat shows.

When things are going well between people there is synchronicity in their behaviour.[4] The dancing metaphor sums it up well - we naturally match the movements of our dancing partner, but we don't tend to dance with people we don't like. Mismatching sends out the message 'I'm different from you, we have nothing in common.' When people identify with each other, they cooperate. One of the principle ways we identify with one another is by giving out similar signals that say, in effect, 'This person is like me, I can get along with them.'

Rapport with a difficult person

It has been said that as we speak 93 per cent of the interaction is non-verbal. Words contribute a mere 7 per cent to the communication, the extra-verbal factors in our speech (tone, intensity, speed, volume and so on) represent 38 per cent, and body language (position, movements, gestures, breathing and changes in our physiology) make up the remaining 55 per cent. Whether we accept these figures at face value or not - and quite obviously there would be slight variations from depending on the person or the circumstances[5] - it is easy to see that the general proportions are about right. We can all think of times when someone has communicated something 'loud and clear' to us without ever saying a word. In a telling example I once witnessed in a supermarket, the mother of a small boy roughly tugged on his arm to pull him towards her as she bent her face towards his and spat: 'I am not angry, all right?' I doubt that the boy believed the words that were so wildly at odds with the non-verbal language – much safer to go with the 93 per cent that said she was angry than the 7 per cent that claimed she was not.

When dealing with a difficult person it is useful to be aware of the skill of non-verbal rapport building. Matching the person, as I have described, is an immediate and accessible way to demonstrate to them that we are interested in working with them rather than confronting them. The aim is not to match their difficult behaviour, of course, but to convey, at an unconscious level, that we are not a threat, thereby working towards engendering trust and confidence in us.

Checklist: rapport-building

1. Notice how the other person is sitting or standing and roughly 'mirror' their body position. Aim for symmetry rather than copying them.

2. Do the same with their movements. For example, one person may gesticulate when they are speaking, another might stand with their hands in their pockets. Doing something to match these patterns of behaviour helps the process.

3. The same ideas apply for voice, speech, breathing, eye contact and so on.

4. Don't aim to match all of them - it is best to go for the largest part of the message (the body language). Once that has been mastered, try pacing their speech and reproduce it in your conversations with them. Nevertheless, pay attention to other facets because they provide vital information. For example, breathing and the volume of their voice can tell you a lot about their emotional state.

5. Remember, too, that any interaction between people involves not just speaking and moving but also silences, stillness, thinking times and dozens of other behavioural components that we can reproduce with subtlety.

6. If you deal with people on the telephone, this non-verbal process still occurs. You may not have the advantage of seeing the other person, but to compensate you can hear far

more detail (remember they can too), since when we are on the telephone we have a sensitive microphone a few centimetres from our mouth. It also appears that people can 'hear' a smile so we should not assume that the apparently 'invisible' aspects of behaviour are not present.

If you are uncertain about using any of the techniques, wait until you have become more confident through observing the interactions of others. I must also emphasise that this is not a 'bolt-on accessory' aimed at coercion or manipulation. It is an acknowledged part of human relationships[6] and as such it happens naturally. Any attempts to force it or use it insincerely will damage, rather than enhance, rapport as the other person will pick up on it unconsciously even if they don't consciously register that something is wrong.

Chapter 8
Attacks, demands and put-downs

I have categorised difficult behaviour into seven 'types', each one outlining a constellation of habits that we find hard to deal with. The following two chapters will tell you about them and offer some constructive suggestions for handling them.

Four of these 'characters' use openly antagonistic, demanding or aggressive behaviour and so are readily identifiable as difficult. The Steamroller tries to flatten us; the Guerrilla uses hostile sniping tactics; the Critical Complainer uses 'justified' attacks and the Expert withers us with superiority and put-downs while pushing through their own agenda. These four are all practised in the use of hostile behaviour.

On the other hand, not all difficult behaviour is so visible and immediately recognisable. Chapter 9 demonstrates how the Shadow can be difficult to pin down, how the Silent Type's quiet passivity often gets our goat and how the Grouser's constant negativity would try the patience of a saint.

Working titles, not labels

A word of warning: these titles are designed to make it easier to describe the various behaviours involved. They are working titles and not meant to be used as labels. I would not encourage anyone to believe that the world is really peopled by Steamrollers, Guerrillas and Grousers. In fact, as we have already seen, making judgements in this way only hinders our thought processes when dealing with difficult behaviour. The titles I have given to these seven types are merely for the purposes of identification, to enable me to describe the approaches which I recommend. Indeed, few people will fall neatly into any of the categories. Some people use a variety of behaviours that don't fit into a single category, others may change over time.

Under stress we regress

Planning a course of action to be used when we meet difficult behaviour is a vital first step. But how can we be sure we'll remember what we've planned or be able to execute it when we need it?

A number of years ago I was speaking to a firefighter who, after 20 years in the service, was suddenly suffering from what had been diagnosed as post-traumatic stress disorder (PTSD).[1]

'I know what the problem is,' he told me. 'I've been walking into blazing buildings for 20 years, and every time my head was saying "Go in there" and my feet were saying "Get the hell out of here". I wanted to run but I had a job to do.'

When I asked him how he had managed so well for so many years he said, 'Training', adding, by way of explanation: 'We drill for skill because under stress we regress.'

In many situations where people are expected to function well and consistently under pressure, repeated training is used as a way of helping them to turn the planned programme of actions into a strategy. To be really effective this training will simulate something of the conditions of the real incident. Firefighters, airline pilots, soldiers and many others are trained in this way. The army, for example, knows that if it is to prepare frontline troops properly for the heat of battle or the support team for the demands on them back at base, then that training must simulate something of the stress of the real event. Mark Dawes, a former Royal Navy officer now working a personal safety trainer, explains: 'A huge failing in interpersonal skills training is that it is taught in a safe and predictable environment where individuals are not challenged either emotionally or physically. Therefore, when they are confronted with an individual or situation which challenges their emotional state they fail to execute the skills effectively.'

Planning a course of action is a vital first step, but it is not enough. Even our best-laid plans will not work for us if we if we have not prepared some sort of strategy, an automatic sequence of steps that we'll engage in at the critical time, to get us through the situation. Under normal conditions - sitting quietly on the bus or at home - thinking about what we'll say to so-and-so the next time they try it on, it all seems perfectly clear. In our fantasies we can all become Oscar Wilde or Ruby Wax, primed and ready with the perfect quip or response. Our imaginations know exactly what we'll say the next time a Guerrilla says 'Can't you take a joke?' or a Shadow tries to wheedle some information out of us with flattery. But in reality, relying on our creativity or inspiration at such times is at best a shaky strategy and at worst a hopeless one.

Success with people or situations we have found difficult is more likely when we have prepared our strategy and practised it. The next two chapters show some do's and don'ts, and some of the key points and principles people have found so useful in moving things forward.

THE STEAMROLLER

The type of difficult behaviour that people generally find the most challenging is the Steamroller. Their hostile and intimidating outbursts are threatening and even frightening. In the front line of public service, this is one of the most common types of difficult behaviour that people have to deal with: rude and angry members of the public making demands in an unreasonable way. And it's not just limited to customers or service users, it is also a frighteningly common tactic used by some managers towards their own staff! Time and again when

I am running courses on dealing with difficult people or conflict management I am asked for advice on dealing with this type of bullying tactic when it is delivered by a manager.

Wherever it is coming from, even the most resourceful of us will get worn down pretty quickly when faced with people who act in this way. It may be face-to-face or it may be on the telephone. The tactics are the same and so are the strategies for dealing with it.

A Steamroller will flatten you if you give them the opportunity. In an attempt to control the environment around them - to make things happen, as they would see it - they adopt a superior air and appear arrogant, demanding and impatient. They ask a lot of questions, like 'What's the matter with you?', 'Don't you ever listen to me?' and 'Do I have to do everything around here?'

This is not because they are interested in answers. Asking questions in this way is almost guaranteed to wrong-foot the other person. In the same way that a boxer in the ring knows that the all-important first punch will determine the outcome of the match, Steamroller behaviour sends its target reeling in such a way that they find it difficult to marshal their resources and respond in an articulate way. Steamrollers' blaming behaviour is designed to break their victim down - if they keep on the attack maybe no one will notice how insecure and exposed they feel. The Steamroller's overriding aim seems to be to get their own way and they act as though that's all they're interested in. In fact their behaviour is frequently driven by uncertainty, insecurity and doubt. They are attempting to make themselves feel safer and more in control through their behaviour.

If you listen carefully to the language that the Steamroller uses you might find clues to what is really going on. For example, statements like 'Nobody ever listens to me' and 'Do I have to do everything around here?' tell us - if we can step back from the bluff and bluster - something about what the person is feeling.

But before we get into trying to understand this difficult behaviour we have to think about acceptable behaviour. We all have the right to express our dissatisfaction towards others, whether this complaint is about goods, services we have received (or haven't), or someone's behaviour towards us. We don't have the right (and neither do they, of course) to threaten, insult, intimidate, worry or in any other way impose ourselves on the other person. It is not the complaint that is the problem, it is the way in which it is delivered. The first thing to remember when dealing with a steamroller is that, whatever their complaint or demand, it is the *behaviour* which is out of order and which must be stopped.

Steamrollers also frequently use intimidating body language as well as verbal interaction. Invading our space, punctuating their remarks with finger-pointing and table-banging or hands-on-the-hips posturing are just some of the ways they seem to puff themselves up to appear more intimidating.

People often refer to this as bullying behaviour, which of course it is in that the Steamroller wants to push or cajole the other person into responding in the way they want. By extension, people I have spoken to in organisations have often referred to those who use Steamroller tactics as bullies. We need to be careful about this sort of rash - though perfectly natural - labelling. Just because we don't like someone else's behaviour it should not automatically qualify them as a bully. Bullying involves difficult behaviour, of course, but what distinguishes a bully from someone who becomes difficult is that the bully has an agenda: a systematic and committed strategy of doing emotional damage to another person.

Typical Steamroller characteristics

- Aggressive and hostile
- Want their own way
- Need to control their environment
- Talk loudly and often interrupt

- Brash and insistent
- Do not seem to listen well
- Use bullying behaviour (though they are they are not necessarily bullies).

The Steamroller in action

Scene: a doctor's receptionist is confronted by an irate patient

RECEPTIONIST: Good morning, can I help you?

PATIENT: Yes, I have an appointment to see Dr Root.

RECEPTIONIST: Dr Root is in a meeting at the moment. Can I have your name, please?

PATIENT: Martin, and my appointment is for 10.30. She won't keep me waiting, I hope?

RECEPTIONIST: [checking diary] You aren't on the list Mr Martin, are you sure you have an appointment?

PATIENT: [raising his voice] Sure? Of course I'm sure. I called yesterday and spoke to Dr Root in person. We arranged a meeting for today.

RECEPTIONIST: Well, I don't have any record of it here [still checking through diary].

PATIENT: Where is she? Let me speak to her personally! What is your job here anyway? Get me someone who can sort this out!

RECEPTIONIST: I've already told you, she's with someone at the moment.

PATIENT: And I've already told you, we have arranged an appointment for today at 10.30. Interrupt her!

RECEPTIONIST: [looking helpless] I don't think your attitude...

PATIENT: How long have you been working here? I've been dealing with Dr Root for years now. I've never been messed about like this before. Just you wait until she hears about this, your feet won't touch the ground, you'll be out of here so fast...

RECEPTIONIST: There must be some mistake... I'm sure...
PATIENT: The mistake was the day they started employing people like you. You've not heard the last of this! [storms out]
RECEPTIONIST: Well, what a nerve! How could I let him get away with that?

What went wrong?

Remember, the issue in a case like this is not whether Mr Martin does or does not have an appointment. The first and most important aspect of this interaction is that his behaviour is out of order. He is disrespectful, rude and insulting. He must be stopped. I know this is easier said than done when people lay into us like this, which is why the first thing you need is a strategy. The moment you become aware of difficult behaviour it should act as a trigger to warn you to respond rather than react: take your time, pay attention to your breathing, body position and how you might appear to the other person. Develop your strategy along the lines below and remember, the aim is not to point-score, put them in the wrong or in any way 'win'. This will only disadvantage you.

Remember, when dealing with a Steamroller:

DO

- Stand firm. If they are standing, you stand – match their body language
- Avoid an argument – you won't win
- Use soothing words, open body language and non-threatening gestures. If you want them to sit down demonstrate this with a 'soft command' gesture of the hand (palm open and upwards, the hand extended towards the chair) and stop talking to give them time to comply

- Stick to the point – they may throw in personal insults, so just agree with what is factual and ignore the rest

- Remain cool – control your need to retaliate. Steamrollers are expert button-pushers – they love to get us shouting at them and weaken our defences in that way

- Acknowledge what they say – tell them you take the facts seriously

- Let them know that you value their opinions in so far as they are factual

- Tell them if you disagree with them: say something like, 'I don't share that point of view', and then ask for more information to continue the conversation in a constructive way

- Engineer a break for yourself, if possible. Find a plausible reason to leave the room and get away from their steamrolling behaviour – to change direction, go and look at your notes, or make a call to check out the veracity of their claims.

DON'T

- Let them interrupt you – which they frequently do. Simply say their name, eg 'Mr Smith, you interrupted me', and then continue. If they interrupt you a second time you say, 'Mr Smith, you interrupted me again.' Make a simple statement of fact unemotionally and avoid making the tone of that 'again' sound too angry or accusatory. It will just lead to more retaliations

- Get into a fight. You won't win and besides, the aim is to bring the conversation to a close and move on, or to turn it into a more balanced and respectful interaction

- Try to point-score, however tempting it might be

- Get drawn into answering those 'Why?' questions or justifying yourself.

How to deal effectively with a Steamroller

RECEPTIONIST: Good morning, can I help you?

PATIENT: Yes, I have an appointment to see Dr Root.

RECEPTIONIST: Dr Root is in a meeting at the moment, could I have your name, please?

PATIENT: Martin, and my appointment is for 10.30. She won't keep me waiting, I hope?

RECEPTIONIST: She's pretty punctual as a rule. Please take a seat and I'll check [indicates chair, starts check appointment book].

PATIENT: [sits down a little reluctantly]

RECEPTIONIST: [checking diary] Mr Martin, I don't have a note of your appointment in the diary... are you sure it is for today?

PATIENT: [immediately stands up] Sure? Of course I'm sure. I called yesterday and spoke to Dr Root in person. We arranged a meeting for today at 10.30.

RECEPTIONIST: Then let me check again... [still checking through diary]

PATIENT: Check again, check again... Where is she? Let me speak to her personally!

RECEPTIONIST: Ah! Here it is, your appointment...

PATIENT: [interrupting] How long have you been working here? I've been dealing with Dr Root for years now. I've never been messed about like this before. Just you wait until she hears about this, your feet won't touch the ground, you'll be out of here so fast...

RECEPTIONIST: [stands up slowly and non-threateningly] Mr Martin, you interrupted me. I have found your appointment – it is for tomorrow at 10.30.

PATIENT: Tomorrow! I clearly remember making the appointment for the 26th. Stop trying to cover up your mistakes...

RECEPTIONIST: Mr Martin, the 26th is tomorrow, today is the 25th....

PATIENT: Now just...

RECEPTIONIST: Please, Mr Martin, you interrupted me again. I was just going to say – so that you don't have a wasted journey – please take a seat for a moment while I see how I can help [checking diary]. I think I can get you an appointment in about twenty minutes. How would that be?

PATIENT: Well, it's better than nothing I suppose...

RECEPTIONIST: And I'll get a message to her so that she knows that you are here [walks off].

PATIENT: [sits calmly]

Putting the strategy into action

The receptionist knew her strategy, which allowed her to take control from the outset. She did not get into a competition with Mr Martin, try to talk over him or put him in his place. By indicating the chair and inviting him to sit down she set the tone for the discussion and by sitting (at least at first) he tacitly complied with this. She also pointed out when he had interrupted. This was not an admonishment, simply a statement which says: 'I cannot speak and sort this out while you are speaking over me, so please stop.'

When he stood up, so did she (see non-verbal rapport-building on page 120). Some people worry that this might make things worse. If done calmly it does not. The idea is to match the other person's body position, not mirror their aggressive behaviour. (Incidentally, should he escalate this aggressive behaviour to an attack, she is better placed to move quickly from a standing position than if seated.)

The question I am always asked, of course, is: 'Ah yes, but he was in the wrong, he had turned up a day early for his appointment. What would have happened if he had been right, and the receptionist (or the organisation) had got it wrong?' Well, that doesn't change anything. The problem here is the man's behaviour (the process), not the appointment (the content). The receptionist's first job is to state the terms of the discussion (sit down, don't interrupt etc), in order to calm the patient's behaviour, so that the question of the appointment can be discussed. The interaction should not be based on who is 'right' and who is 'wrong' (we all think we are right when we are on the defensive, don't we?).

As for the appointment and which day it was for, as well as the receptionist's suggestion of slotting him in 20 minutes later, these are operational issues which will vary from situation to situation. For example, let's assume that Mr Martin had turned up on the right day (it was the organisation that had got it wrong) and there was no possibility of finding him an appointment. Then the receptionist would have to apologise for the error (an expression of regret, not an admission of guilt).[2] In either case the Steamroller behaviour is what is at issue here, not mistakes or misunderstandings due to the patient or the administration.

THE GUERRILLA

Like the Steamroller, the Guerrilla also uses hostile and aggressive behaviour, but less overtly. These people aren't brave enough to stand up and say they're being unpleasant. But they can often seem harder to deal with because their attacks are covert and come under the guise of good-natured jokes. They can make us question our own judgement, maybe we were wrong – after all, weren't they only joking? In fact, when tackled about their behaviour the Guerilla's standard defence is 'You're too sensitive' or 'Can't you take a joke?'

This is one of the most pernicious and damaging behaviours we see in the workplace. Because the Guerrilla's attacks and jibes masquerade as humour, people tend to unwittingly condone and support them. The supposed light-heartedness of the comments makes them difficult to counter head-on because they make the victim (or target, if you prefer) seem petty for mentioning it. After all, anybody with a normal sense of humour can take a joke, can't they?

In real life

When Steve joined the Mental Health Care Team he noticed that Carol, one of the longer serving team members, often made jibes and jokes publicly at another colleague's expense. The target was Sanjit, who went quietly and efficiently about his work but almost anything he did seemed to attract jokey comments and snide remarks from Carol. Being new to the job Steve, like others before him no doubt, accepted this as part of the way things were and he even joined in the laughter from time to time.

Several months into the job, Steve came into the common room for the regular staff meeting. As usual, Carol was holding centre stage as the various team members came in, helped themselves to coffee and settled into their places. She finished a short tirade against the government of the day with the usual sort of tangential remark aimed in Sanjit's direction: 'I don't suppose you agree, do you Sanjit? You probably voted for this bloody lot. In fact, it's all your fault.'

In his usual way, Sanjit did not answer but gave a strained attempt at a smile. Steve, by this time sitting directly opposite Sanjit, said: 'Leave it out Carol, enough's enough.' 'Leave it out?' said Carol. 'Can't he take a joke? Anyway, what business is it of yours? Sanjit can speak for himself, can't he?' She had not liked being challenged.

'And I can speak for myself,' said Steve. 'You're always on at him, it's almost like bullying. Just leave him alone.'

Carol's response was to flush deep red, stand up and stride out of the room. She was too insulted, she said, to be able to attend the meeting. During the staff meeting Steve made a point of mentioning that he had been uncomfortable with Carol's behaviour for some time and had felt guilty of complicity but had not known how to tackle it with her. Other team members expressed similar views.

Later that day Steve met up with Carol and explained that he had not wanted to upset her. She was a fairly dominant person in the team, he said, and perhaps did not realise the full impact of her remarks. She should not take either Sanjit's response or that of the team to mean that such put-downs were acceptable.

Carol managed to maintain her state of high dudgeon for a week or so and studiously avoided Steve as far as possible. She continued to make asides and unwanted comments about life in general (and for a few weeks about Steve in particular, as long as he was not in range), but Sanjit was now spared her remarks.

'I never expected to change her,' said Steve. 'I just felt ashamed that I was guilty by association with her remarks.'

In telling the story above, the question I often ask of groups is: 'How many people were involved in Carol's behaviour?' In such situations silence can be seen as tacit approval of the unwanted behaviour, so anyone who does not speak up against it is at least permitting it to happen, even if they are not actively encouraging it. I have used this example to show how this happens, rather than the strategy for dealing with it. If Sanjit could have taken appropriate action sooner perhaps things would not have built up to the point where it took an explosion to clear the air.

Typical Guerrilla characteristics:

- Using sniping tactics, criticising your behaviour or decisions by making jokes about you publicly to other people, or behind your back
- Playing to the audience – they make their victims look foolish
- Denying they are using difficult behaviour and instead turn it back on the victim, saying that it was only meant as a joke

- Going underground, act hurt or step up their difficult behaviour when tackled.

The Guerrilla in action

Scene: Laura is giving a report to colleagues on the training programme budget. Paul is part of the group she is addressing.

LAURA: Well, I've finally got all the details together and done the calculations on how much we've spent from the training budget.

PAUL: We've been waiting so long for these details we thought you'd gone to Brazil with the money! [laughter]

LAURA: You'll be pleased to know that we have still got a substantial part of the budget left for more training this year.

PAUL: Good. Perhaps we can send someone on a course for preparing accounts quickly [laughter].

LAURA: We've only spent half as much so far this year as we had by the same time last year...

PAUL: That's because some of us have been working twice as hard – we haven't had any time for training.

LAURA: I've done my best to check all the details properly... I thought... [voice trembling] I'll type up the figures and circulate them by the end of the week.

What went wrong?

This is a very difficult situation, partly because it is so public. Paul is hiding behind the group to deliver his unpleasant remarks and Laura, already uncertain and nervous about speaking in front of the group, is not likely to have the courage or presence of mind to tackle his behaviour. She knows all too well (or at least believes) that any response she might make will be used as fuel to Paul's sharp wit. She rightly recognises that she is no match for him.

Indeed, any attempt to parry with Paul would only

reinforce the behaviour: she would be joining in and thereby condoning it. This does not mean she would be approving, but she would be sending the message to Paul and the others present that such behaviour is OK really. Clearly it is not. Paul needs to be told in no uncertain terms that his behaviour is unacceptable.

Looking at things from Paul's point of view for a moment, it might be that his comments are justified. Maybe he has a valid grievance, perhaps Laura was late with the accounts and has caused difficulties elsewhere as a result. Once again, it is not the remarks that are incorrect but the way in which the information is delivered. If Paul has a message for Laura about the quality of her work – and his position relative to her justifies it – he is perfectly entitled to tell her. However, in the circumstances described here, she will be more likely to hear it as an attack rather than a valid observation about her working habits.

One of the difficulties here is the public context of the remarks. Challenging Paul in front of the group is difficult and, since it threatens him with loss of face, a high-risk strategy. This does not mean I would not use it, in fact I recommend it. First, though, I suggest a more discreet attempt to point out that his behaviour is not helping either of them, providing an opportunity for him to give the information in a more appropriate setting (see *How to deal pivately with a Guerilla*, below). If that fails then he has left himself open to the sort of public humiliation he has been inflicting on his target. Try some of the strategies listed below in the first instance.

Remember, when dealing with a Guerrilla:

DO

- Get them alone, if possible, to disempower them
- Say something positive to disarm them and build a little

rapport before tackling them

- Tackle their covert attacks head-on. Say something like: 'You know Nigel, it was really funny what you said but I thought I sensed a criticism, did I?' and then wait for the reply. There is a more than 90 per cent chance that the person will say 'Well, no.'
- Tell them that if they ever do have a criticism of you, you would much prefer that they say it directly to you in future
- If a Guerrilla's remarks are relayed to you by someone else, get the other person's permission to quote them, to ensure corroboration and accuracy. Go back to the offending Guerrilla with the information and follow the steps above. Again, tell the person that in future if they have anything to say that concerns you, they should say it directly to you. That way you can deal with it
- Repeat the same approach if they start their games with you again. Guerrilla behaviour is usually quite an ingrained habit that may not be broken the first time around. Make it clear, in an unemotional way, that you find their behaviour unacceptable.

DON'T:

- Join in the laughter at their remarks
- Ignore the behaviour or pretend it isn't happening
- Take part in the game and try and reply with a quip. You risk turning Guerrilla behaviour into open warfare.

How to deal privately with a Guerrilla:

My recommended strategy is as follows:

- Make an appointment to see the Guerrilla, call them up or if you bump into them ask if you can have a few minutes of their time later. Although you might be tempted to discuss things straight away, resist the urge. Suggest a meeting later that day or in a day or two. This allows them time to wonder what you want and it will work in your favour. Remember how you have felt if someone told you they wanted to see you but did not say why.

- Make sure any appointment is not in your office and tell them it will only take a couple of minutes. It is essential that the meeting is brief and that you can end it by leaving (difficult if they have come to you).

- Turn up at precisely the appointed time. Thank them for coming, use a little chit-chat as an ice-breaker and make sure they understand that you have only a few minutes but that it is really important for you to have this time with them (you are restating that the meeting will be brief but letting them know that 'brief' does not mean unimportant). Take a minute or two to let them know, indirectly, that this is a non-threatening situation.

- Turn the conversation to the time of the last offensive remarks. Be specific about when this was, but don't go into detail (and avoid the sort of blanket statement such as 'Every time we are in a meeting...')

- Say something like 'I know your remarks generally go down well with people', or 'You have a natural gift for humour...' which acknowledges their popularity. They probably need some reassurance. Confident people don't need to use Guerrilla tactics.

- Switching to the first person, use 'I' statements to let them know how the remarks affected you: 'The trouble is, I was put right off my stride', or 'It felt to me like an attack.'

- They will probably attempt a few of those 'It was only a joke' type of comments. There's no need to respond to these with anything more than a simple acknowledgement like 'Uh-huh' or 'Oh, I see.'

- Then tell them that, if in future they have anything to say to you about your work, you would much prefer them to say it to you directly (and in private). Explain that if they do you'll be able to get the message rather than feeling uncertain about what was meant and be able to do something in response to it.

• Thank them for their time and leave.

At all costs avoid getting drawn back into the conversation at this point otherwise they might well try a little verbal grooming to smooth things over and put you off your guard. Then they'll find some way of sticking it to you again. If they try to raise the subject of a genuine complaint they have against you ('But you really were late with the accounts'), tell them you really can't stay to talk about it now but that you are keen to discuss it another time. Suggest a meeting but don't get caught up looking for a suitable time or waiting while they check their diary. If you take up a new topic now the whole purpose of your carefully prepared meeting will be lost.

I have known situations where this strategy worked like a charm. In one case a female accounts manager told me about a colleague she had known since they were at school together. 'The trouble is,' she said, 'whenever we are in a meeting he mentions an incident from our childhood. It was no big deal but it is inappropriate and it embarrasses me.' This had been going on, she said, for 'close on 20 years'. She finally tackled him, in private, as I suggest above, and to her pleasure and amazement he responded very positively, explaining that he was intending to show others that they went back a long way and that it was a relationship he valued, as it set them apart from other colleagues. 'He apologised profusely and never made the comments again,' she said.

However, you may not be so lucky with your Guerrilla. I suggest you give the private meeting approach a couple of tries, and remember that it may take a little time for them to relinquish old habits, so don't be too hard on them. This is particularly true if the offender is male – men tend to use this sort of banter as a bonding ritual and some don't realise when they have gone too far or when the setting makes it inappropriate.[3]

If – having tried your best by tackling this sensitive topic in private – the Guerilla persists with their unwanted asides and distractions, then tackling them publicly is justified.

How to deal publicly with a Guerrilla

LAURA: Well, I've finally got all the details together and done the calculations on how much we've spent from the training budget...

PAUL: We've been waiting so long for these details we thought you'd gone to Brazil with the money! [laughter]

LAURA: You'll be pleased to know that we have still got a substantial part of the budget left for more training this year...

PAUL: Good. Perhaps we can send someone on a course for preparing accounts quickly [laughter].

LAURA: We've only spent half as much so far this year as we had by the same time last year...

PAUL: That's because some of us have been working twice as hard – we haven't had any time for training.

LAURA: Excuse me, Paul, I know you're getting laughs from everyone, but it sounds to me as if you're having a go at me. Is that right? [silence from Paul: she turns her attention back to the group] You'll be pleased to know that there's still a substantial amount of the budget left for more training.

PAUL: [a little more quietly and looking round for support from the group] I'd be pleased to know how that's going to do me any good now.

LAURA: I'm sorry about this, everybody, but Paul seems to think that speed is all that matters when it comes to managing the training budget. I like to check things thoroughly, as I believe accuracy is more important than speed. Is there anyone else who shares Paul's view that I have taken too long? [silence]

OK. Since we've got a substantial part of the budget left, there's plenty of money left over for the individual training requests we've been receiving from staff members. I'll type up the figures and circulate them by the end of the week, so those requests can be considered at the next meeting.

Putting the strategy into action

This approach may not seem to be the best way to win friends and influence people, but surprisingly few people are offended by it. Maintaining courtesy and respect for the Guerrilla helps them save face; it also wins the respect of the group, which the offender will recognise. Since they need the group on their side they are not eager to risk appearing boorish by publicly continuing the challenge in the face of a cool and respectful response from the speaker. In the example above, Laura persistently and good-naturedly challenges each intrusion, finally resorting to the old public speaker's ruse for dealing with hecklers: she throws it back to the crowd.

The Guerrilla may sulk, they may go 'underground' and simply gossip behind your back. The best strategy in such cases is to ignore it in the first instance. If it persists and you hear about it, then presumably there must be some 'well-meaning' third party reporting it to you.

Dealing with reports of Guerrilla attacks

How do you respond to reports by one person that someone else has had a go at you? This 'Guerrilla by proxy' behaviour can be almost as problematic as the public kind of attack described above. It is even harder to go to the person who is supposed to have made the remarks and deal with them. Are the comments accurate? What was their context? Has the 'reporter' taken them as jibes when no harm was intended? More importantly perhaps, certainly in the first instance, who is really the Guerrilla? It may well be the person who is credited with making the remarks, but equally it could be the person who delivered them to you. After all, why would a 'friend' need to bring you down with someone else's negative comments?

In such situations I recommend an immediate and very direct response.

When the person comes to you and reports the negative comments made by someone else about you:

- Acknowledge their good intent by saying something like 'Well, I'm sure you meant well, but this now means I shall have to deal with it', and be sure to add: 'Can I quote you on that?' They will probably back-pedal furiously, trying to avoid having their name mentioned.

- Explain to them gently that there may be something of importance in the remarks and that, anyway, you would like to tell the Guerrilla: 'If you have anything to say to another person about my work I would much prefer that you said it to me directly in future.'

- Let the person who brought you the news know that, if you can't quote them, your comments might appear to be based on 'idle tittle-tattle or gossip', so you really need to use their name.

- There are two possible courses of action here. The first is that you go back to the perpetrator and follow the steps previously described for dealing with a Guerrilla, quoting the source of your information if they challenge you

- The second possible course of action is that you go through the same steps, but because you sense that your source is frightened of reprisals by the Guerrilla you protect them and do not mention their name.

In this scenario, there are two people who need to get the message. The gossip will hear from you straight away that their habit is going to rebound on them and by using the phrase 'tittle-tattle or gossip' you have let them know how you regard their intrusive behaviour. The Guerrilla will also learn that they can no longer make these idle, back-stabbing remarks in safety – you will always come back to them. No longer able to hide behind anonymity the Guerrilla should think twice before having a go again.

There are two important provisos when considering Guerrilla behaviour:

1. There may be some truth in the Guerrilla's remarks, even though the method of delivery is unpleasant and unprofessional. Consider that you may have something to learn from them.

2. Sniping, back-biting and complaining are very common when an organisation is in difficulty or going through change. For many people these behaviours are coping strategies for dealing with uncertainty or low morale. In such cases, rather than seeing Guerrilla behaviour left, right and centre, it is more useful to regard it as a symptom of distress or low morale. The remedy here should be applied to the organisation, rather than the individual.

THE CRITICAL COMPLAINER

Critical Complainers are the people who constantly find fault with everything. They can have different degrees of impact depending on the nature of our relationship with them. Those who have some power over us, such as a complaining boss or a critical supervisor, are likely to be more damaging to our self-esteem because their complaints tend to include accusations about us or how we do our work. For those of us who work with the public – since the customer is always right – Critical Complainers can be pretty troublesome as well, though when they are handled correctly they can usually be headed off before they start getting personal.

Whatever the complaint, when the Critical Complainer comes in to present it they've already built up a pretty good head of steam. What generally happens is that we sense that the steam is about to blow and we react accordingly, by trying to play it down or deny or ignore their complaint.

This is precisely the opposite of what is required. It is completely natural to attempt to pacify someone or to try and protect ourselves by 'pushing away' what we perceive as their attack. Unfortunately, this has the effect of getting the Critical Complainer to step up their demands, rather than calm down, go away or leave us alone. More usefully the steps to follow are:

- Give them your full attention
- Adopt 'open' body language
- Listen attentively and invite more information
- Summarise your understanding of their complaint
- Find out what they would like to have happen (What do they want? This may not be the same as what they are asking for).

Think about what it is that any of us wants when we are complaining. Of course, we want to get a result, but underlying that there is something more fundamental. We want recognition, rather than denial, that our complaint is valid. If the complaint is about something specific (bad service or faulty goods, for example), we probably want compensation or a replacement. If it is about someone's behaviour (they treat us badly or their work is not up to the mark), we are more likely to want to see some sign or acknowledgement that things are going to be different in future. Underlying both of these situations is our need to feel that our complaints are heard. In other words, before any specific actions are taken to satisfy our complaint, it is absolutely paramount that we feel that the other person is listening to us, taking us seriously, and in some way letting us know that they are understanding where we are coming from. We want some sign, recognition or validation of our claims, rather than a response that says, in effect, that we do not exist.

The complaint is not about the complaint...

Since the first thing most people want when they have a grievance is to be taken seriously, the standard procedure for dealing with complaints is to show that we are listening. This does not just mean paying attention to the complainer, we also have to demonstrate that we have heard. Many people think that in order to respond to a complaint they have to be able to give the complainer what they want. This may be fine if you can, but in many situations you may be unable to supply, say, a hospital bed for someone's mother or a place on a train that has been cancelled. In fact, in many, many situations where staff are expected to deal with complainers they are unable to give what is wanted. They feel disempowered and are unsure of how to deal with people who make demands in this way and they fear, often rightly, that the complaints will turn critical and personal.

So we need a strategy that does not rely on appeasement. Coming back to the fundamental human need to be recognised and taken seriously, the first rule in dealing with someone who is complaining is to acknowledge that we take it seriously. Conversely, many people who complain do so because of past grievances, because they do not feel as if they have been heard. Not surprisingly, they then step up their demands (or the way they make them). They may become more demanding, louder, more threatening or extreme in some other way. At this point they start to add criticism to their complaints. They may become personal and very insulting. The skill in dealing with them is to intervene before they get to this stage. If it is too late, and they are already rude and insulting when they get to you (see 'The Steamroller' on page 127), remember that it is perfectly legitimate for them to have a complaint and they are entitled to voice it. However, they are not entitled to be rude, disrespectful or insulting in presenting their complaint. As I have mentioned before, it is not the complaint that is the problem, it is the way in which it is delivered.

Typical Critical Complainer characteristics

- Can be personal in their attacks
- Are always on the look-out for things going wrong, so they can wade in with a criticism
- Usually find that things are not up to their (often unattainable) standards
- Their 'complaint' is often about something else.

The Critical Complainer in action

Scene: a client held up in a waiting room

CLIENT: Excuse me, I'd like to know what's going on, please?
EMPLOYEE: Sorry?
CLIENT: I have already been here almost an hour, and I have seen several people who arrived after me called for their appointments! Parking round here is terrible, and you haven't even got a coffee machine. And there's not a magazine or a newspaper to be seen.
EMPLOYEE: An hour? That would surprise me, just sit and wait and you'll be called as soon as someone is free to see you.
CLIENT: Sit and wait? I have been waiting for an hour! And it was the same last week, there doesn't seem to be any action around here.
EMPLOYEE: Look, we are very busy, as you can see. You are not the only member of the public here, we have to consider everyone [going back to her reading].
CLIENT: [controlled] I know I'm not the only person here, and that's all the more reason for you to remember that we are the customers, the people who pay your wages. I've a good

mind to cancel my business here and go somewhere else.
EMPLOYEE: [still looking down] Well, that's your choice, of
course. It's a free world.
CLIENT: We'll see about that! [storms out]

What went wrong?

This staff member really got off on the wrong foot. Instead of
respectfully acknowledging the client's presence he launched
straight into a who's-right-and-who's-wrong tussle by
challenging the client's statement that she had been waiting an
hour. From then on it went from bad to worse.

Remember, when dealing with a Critical Complainer:

DO

- Greet them cordially. Look friendly and smile – it throws
  them slightly off their beat and demonstrates that you are
  there to help
- Listen non-defensively to them and check back that you
  have understood. Stick to the relevant facts only and
  remember to use *when, where, how, what* questions
- Offer a sincere expression of regret for the inconvenience
  they are suffering – tell them that you sympathise – tell
  them, for example, that in their position you would
  probably feel the same
- Ensure that they understand that you want to help. Say
  something like 'I am here to help' or 'I want to sort this out
  for you if I can'. Use appropriate language and do not make
  promises you can't keep. (A statement like 'I want to sort
  this out if I can' acknowledges your intent, it does not
  promise success)
- Keep it brief and to the point. Critical Complainers want

to feel that there is a sense of movement, that something is going to be done about their complaint

- Ask them what their preferred outcome would be; get a factual answer that you can act on – often they simply want to feel acknowledged
- Tell them what you are going to do about it and then do it
- Thank them for bringing the matter to your attention
- Shake hands with them, if it is appropriate to the context.

DON'T

- Challenge their version of events or try to correct them
- Begin to act until you know what they want
- Keep them waiting, or the person you have to deal with will be twice as difficult. (Complainers are often teetering on the brink of blowing up out of control so, whenever possible, deal with them promptly).
- Try and score points by 'putting them in their place'
- Make personal comments about them, even if they get quite personal in their attack on you
- Fail to do what you've promised to do.

How to deal effectively with a Critical Complainer

CLIENT: Excuse me, I'd like to know what's going on, please?
EMPLOYEE: [smiling] Good morning, how can I help?
CLIENT: I have already been here almost an hour, and I have seen several people who arrived after me called for their appointments! Parking round here is terrible, and you haven't even got a coffee machine. And there's not a magazine or a newspaper to be seen.
EMPLOYEE: I'm sorry, we do get snowed under sometimes. I'll look into it right away, what's your name please?
CLIENT: My name? Mrs Watson, but what good is that going to do? I'll still have spent an hour wasting my time.

EMPLOYEE: I sympathise, Mrs Watson. I know how difficult it can be to park around here, and if I'd been kept waiting on top of that I don't think I'd have been as patient as you. Now, you say that you've noticed that some people who arrived after you have in fact been served ahead of you, is that right?

CLIENT: [regaining composure a little] Yes.

EMPLOYEE: Thanks for the suggestions about coffee and the newspapers, by the way, I'll pass it on to our customer services department. About the parking, is your car OK for now? I'm pretty sure I can sort this out if you can give me a few minutes.

CLIENT: I'll be OK for a little longer, just tell me something is going to be done.

EMPLOYEE: Give me five minutes, Mrs Watson, and I'll see if I can put an end to your waiting. If you need to use a phone because you've been held up there's one over on the wall. Thanks for being so understanding.

CLIENT: Thank you [sits down].

Putting the strategy into action

Right from the start this interaction went better. Of course, the staff member here was not obliged to go into such detail about what he called 'suggestions about coffee and the newspapers', but it does demonstrate that he heard everything the client said. He also checked out her parking arrangements – if she is worried about getting a parking ticket, that may interfere with her ability to wait patiently. Along with offering her the use of the telephone, it also demonstrated concern, which is a good rapport-builder.

THE EXPERT

Experts are quick thinkers with lots of good ideas. In their haste they make mistakes but this doesn't put them off. These people have a fully formed opinion on everything. They have an air of superiority and can't see why other people – whether they are simply a bit slower or just don't agree with them – are wasting their time. They can be useful people to have on your side, but frustrating if you want to have equal input.

Experts will frequently have an idea and implement it without checking with those around them. It is as though they don't want to discuss things, they just want to be left alone to do it their way. I believe that this is often because they don't know how to talk about their ideas, and they actually see questions about their plans or projects as challenges rather than a discussion or exchange of information. This may be due to a lack of confidence. This is not always the case by any means – some people are really great self-starters who like working alone – but I have certainly seen cases where people who are unsure about how their ideas will be received tend to get their heads down and finish the job before anyone else can comment. This behaviour may also arise because they do not want to run the risk of having to change anything as a result of input from others, or simply, and less charitably, because they want to have their own way.

Typical Expert characteristics

- They are often very good at their jobs
- They seem unable to discuss a topic and arrive at a consensus. If their attitude doesn't persuade others to do it their way, they tend to withdraw
- They may make snap decisions – often without bothering to check that they have all the information – and consequently make mistakes
- They are not renowned for owning up to their errors or learning from them
- Experts usually blame something, or somebody, else if there is a problem.

The Expert in action

Scene: Mary comes home to find Ron in the kitchen

MARY: What's all that stuff in the hall?

RON: We're going to start decorating the sitting room this weekend. I've got the wallpaper, we already have the paint and all the other stuff we need.

MARY: We? That's the first I've heard about it, we haven't even discussed colours or anything.

RON: Oh Mary, you know we did the other evening. We already have the paint for the woodwork, and the paper I got is the perfect combination, it will look great.

MARY: I just don't get it, why the rush? Can't we take a little more time to agree on things?

RON: What is there to agree? It's obvious that the paper I chose was the best for the job. It'll go perfectly with the paint, and yet it is original and bold enough that we won't get bored with it in six months.

MARY: The paper you got would look OK in a railway waiting room, but not in our sitting room, that pattern is hideous, and I thought we had decided on something in blue to go with the paint, you got pink!

RON: Look, I haven't got time to explain it to you, you know I have a strong sense of colour. Trust me, it'll look great when its finished.

MARY: I could never live with a combination like that except maybe in the toilet or the garden shed where I wouldn't have to spend all my spare time looking at it. Either the paper goes, or I do!

What went wrong?

Mary was surprised to find that, in Ron's mind, the colour scheme for the sitting room had already been decided. Since she lives with him she was probably already aware that he is inclined to drop into Expert mode from time to time and so, recognising the signs in his clipped responses and don't-bother-me-now attitude, she is already primed to react in a way that is likely to make him even less likely to communicate. Responding to this behaviour with demands or signs of frustration only confirms the Expert's view that other people are there to hinder them. At best we'll get a patronising response, at worst a total breakdown of communications. When pushed too hard, they have been known to slam down their tools (or whatever they are working on) and stomp off to their ivory tower with a remark like 'If you don't trust me, do it yourself'.

The key to working with this type of behaviour is what I call the 'Joe Colombo' approach. Remember the TV detective with his wheedlingly patient and studied naiveté? Since Experts act as though they feel superior it can help to play up to that a little (it is less threatening for them to deal with someone who is obviously so ingenuous).

This can be difficult. In effect, by pretending that we share the Expert's delusion about themselves, we temporarily place ourselves lower in the social hierarchy which some people find hard to do. Nevertheless, it pays dividends to use a 'Take me through that again, O Wise One' sort of approach. Experts believe that they are extremely logical and have worked things out, so we have to use a logical approach when checking on their decisions. However, not any old logic will do, it has to be *their* logic.

When dealing with an Expert:

DO

- Be sure you know your subject
- Listen non-defensively and paraphrase their main points back to them
- If they won't listen to your questions or doubts, get them

to explain it to you in such a way that they will spot the errors for themselves

- Keep them to the facts, ask questions which require a yes or no answer
- Use the Expert's knowledge by asking them to predict likely outcomes
- Make relevant and factual statements and stick to the point.

DON'T

- Argue over the details. The Expert probably knows more than you do and if they don't they'll become even more dogmatic and difficult
- Ask them open-ended questions or give them an opportunity to blind you with (their) science
- Take the easy option and give in – they often rely on that. Force them to check through the details with you.

How to deal effectively with an Expert

MARY: What's all that stuff in the hall?

RON: We're going to start decorating the sitting room this weekend. I've got the wallpaper, we already have the paint and all the other stuff we need.

MARY: We? That's the first I've heard about it, we haven't even discussed colours or anything.

RON: Oh Mary, you know we did, the other evening. We already have the paint for the woodwork, and the paper I got is the perfect combination, it will look great.

MARY: Yes, we did discuss it, I just didn't expect you to go ahead so quickly.

RON: [patronisingly] You know what they say dear, 'Time and tide wait for no man.'

MARY: Do you suppose that goes for a woman too? Tell you what, take me through it again. I'm sure you are right, but I need to understand if I'm to be any help. Now, I know the paper is for the walls, obviously. And the paint?

RON: [heaves a sigh and rolls his eyes] The doors and skirtings, of course...

MARY: OK. And I suppose you've already checked the paint and wallpaper together, as they will be when we've finished.

RON: Of course...

MARY: Can you show me? When I've got the whole picture I'll be able to see it as you do. That'll help me a lot.

RON: [sigh] Look, here's the paint, and here is the paper, I chose it to bring out the design... [he turns back to what he is doing]

MARY: [taps him on the shoulder to get his attention] And seeing them together like this, is it as you expected?

RON: Ah!...Well, would you credit it! The lighting in the DIY shop must have been right off. I thought that the paint would bring out the blue flowers in the wallpaper. They never get it right, those big stores!

MARY: We'll we haven't opened it yet, so you can still change it. Tell you what, I'll come with you. We can take the paint with us, that'll overcome the lighting problem.

Putting the strategy into action

Don't be put off by the Expert's mock superiority. Their strategy relies on the fact that we'll probably feel too embarrassed, stupid or worn out to check the detail of their argument. Persist. If you do not understand something, or if you think that they have missed a point, rather than confronting them with demands for information or to point out their errors, go with the flow and get them to check their own facts with you. In other words, get them to explain things from their point of view. If it means swallowing your pride for a short time it will be worth it. And, of course, when you choose a deliberate strategy like this it puts you in control.

Chapter 9
Gossip, silence and negativity

Some difficult behaviour is not immediately recognisable as hostile or aggressive, but its effects may be just as damaging. In this chapter we will look at three 'characters' who use less obvious, more subtle behaviour to push through their own agendas. Again, the titles I have given the types are for identification purposes only – they are not meant to be labels – in order to describe the approaches I recommend for dealing with them.

THE SHADOW

Less charitable people might call the Shadow a gossip or a busybody. They are usually in a job that allows them some freedom to roam around the office, in fact they often seem to shadow everyone else, rather than getting on with their own work. They always know what's going on, who said what to whom and what's happening in the other office. And yet they are always uninvolved, and if you press them about where they got their information they can become vague or mysterious. They know that information is power. They gather and use it in a way that gives them an air of importance – the implication being that only someone of weight would be privy to the facts at their disposal.

Unfortunately, many of the 'facts' that they peddle are only half-true or even totally wrong. When tackled about their wandering ways (perhaps with a suggestion that they spend a little more time doing their work) or confronted about the irrelevance or inaccuracy of some of their remarks, they'll act hurt and shocked. After all, how could anyone accuse them of meddling when all they were trying to do was to share information for the benefit of the company, a colleague, the church or whatever?

The Shadow genuinely has the best interests of the organisation at heart. I have seen both men and women adopting this behaviour and I am firmly convinced that they really do think that, without them, terrible mistakes will be made and the whole organisation will grind to a halt. Though Shadows can be a nuisance, they are often vital and valued members of the team. In some cases it may be that they simply have not kept pace with developments in the organisation. I have known a few 'dinosaurs' who used Shadow behaviour to cover the fact, for example, that they did not really know how to use the new computer system or understand the 'new ways'. It may have been precisely because, in earlier days, they were so good at keeping things running that they were allowed to do things their way. The organisation then realises, too late, that they have become troublesome.

In real life

Leroy had been working in the same organisation for about 20 years. As a draughtsman in an electrical engineering firm his job required a lot of attention to detail and over the years he had become quite indispensable to the department and probably to the company as a whole. Whenever anyone needed to know anything, especially if it was difficult-to-find information such as the number of an obsolete part or a supplier for this-or-that, Leroy knew the answer. If he didn't, he knew someone else who did.

It was one of his regular habits to wander around the offices and plant chatting to all and sundry. Obviously, he also collected a lot of non-essential information, such as who-was-doing-what-to-whom, who was up for retirement and the dates when the company would be closed for Christmas. He was indispensable as an organ of information, a sort of roving newsletter that kept everybody informed about what was going on. But there were problems with this.

Apart from the fact that Leroy didn't get a lot of work done at his desk some days and was often late with his projects, there were two other major inconveniences connected with his behaviour. The first was that a good deal of the 'information' he peddled was little better than idle gossip and frequently inaccurate – hearsay which confused, rather than informed, his audience. Since Leroy clearly possessed a lot of factual information about products and services, people tended to take the other information he gave out as equally reliable, which it wasn't. The second difficulty was that his behaviour threatened the smooth-running of the company. It was easier for a member of staff to 'ask Leroy' than to check the information personally and they tended to use him as a sort of technical enquiry service. This was particularly the case with newer employees, who failed to learn or use the regular channels for keeping themselves informed. As the company grew larger and busier this was potentially putting the business at risk.

Finally, and with difficulty at first, Leroy's manager Harry decided that the Shadow behaviour had to stop.

Realising that Leroy was not malicious, lazy or vindictive and, apart from the frequent absences from his desk, not doing anything that was clearly definable as wrong, Harry was initially at a loss as to how to tackle him about his behaviour. Leroy was always patient and helpful when dealing with enquiries and he definitely had his employer's interests at heart. Harry worried that Leroy, who had been with the company a lot longer than he had, would be offended and take his attempts at 'behaviour modification' badly.

Having called a meeting with Leroy, Harry tackled it head–

on. 'Leroy, I know you are a vital part of this plant, you have been here a lot longer than me and you know more than most of us can ever hope to.' His opener was intended to acknowledge Leroy's importance. 'But I've been increasingly worried lately about two things [keeping it simple]. One, you are getting behind with your work. I really need your output. Two, I am concerned that people are using you as a short-cut to get information which they should be getting via the official route. This may not be too inconvenient for you, but it is not the way we are meant to work. Verbal communications are too prone to misinterpretation and mistakes.'

Having told Leroy what the problem was, Harry concluded:

'Please stick to your own work. I am going to instruct others here to use the technical database for their information searches in future. After all, that is what it is designed for.'

Leroy was at first a little combative about this, defending himself by saying that he only meant to help and that it was not his fault if people sought him out with questions. Harry was reassuring that he would be overseeing the situation and he would discourage intrusions to allow Leroy to get on with his work. Leroy's final question was: 'The database only goes back 10 or 12 years. How will people get the information they need if it is older than that?'

'I shall tell everyone that if they really can't find some vital information then they come to me with a note of what they want,' replied Harry. 'I'll pass it on to you but in a controlled way so that you are not constantly interrupted.' Harry finished by reminding Leroy of his main job and the importance of his work.

I saw Leroy three months later. Everything was running smoothly and he was full of praise for his manager. 'I never really realised there was a problem until it stopped. I was a bit offended at first, but I'm really glad Harry stuck to his guns, and he did protect me. I'd forgotten how good it felt to actually finish a job on time.'

Typical Shadow characteristics

- They always seem to know what's going on in the organisation
- They are masters of vague innuendo and weave a web of rather complicated stories
- You'll have trouble actually seeing a Shadow doing any work. They seem to shadow everyone else
- When confronted with inaccuracies they act hurt and shocked: their defence is that they were only sharing information for the benefit of the company
- They are masters of the 'multiple file' system, hiding what they do in a complex system that only they understand
- They know that if they postpone a decision long enough, there is a good chance it will go away.

The Shadow in action

Scene: Jane, a manager, has requested a piece of information from Shelley, a team member

SHELLEY: Hey Jane! Have you got a moment?
JANE: Hello there, I wanted to see you. How are things going?
SHELLEY: Well, the same as usual, I suppose. Have you heard about Mr Rowe's problem?
JANE: Problem? What problem? What's he been doing?
SHELLEY: It's not so much what he has been doing as what he's not been doing.
JANE: Well, I expect he'll sort it out whatever it is. Now, about that information I asked for...

SHELLEY: Oh, but it's not just him. Janice in Radiography hasn't been able to get any work done for almost two weeks
JANE: Hasn't she? Well, I hope things settle down there soon. Now, about that information I wanted.
SHELLEY: Oh, I've hardly had time with all these disturbances.
JANE: It has been a week since I asked for it. Don't forget, I must have it by Friday.
SHELLEY: Of course, no problem. What's that on your jacket?
JANE: Oh, I was rooting around in the library for some files.
SHELLEY: I've told you before, if you need anything from the library you only have to ask me. You know I am the only one around here who knows where anything is.
JANE: Great, then how about that information I asked for?
SHELLEY: Is that the time? I promised I'd stand in for Mrs Ramsey while she had her eyes tested.

What went wrong?

Jane fell right in with Shelley's strategy of engaging her with irrelevant side issues by asking for more information. She realises her mistake and gets back on track by asking for the information she wants from Shelley, but to no avail. The Shadow is off at another tangent... and so it goes on. The more Jane insists, the more distractions Shelley introduces ('What's that on your jacket?') and finally, when things are getting uncomfortable for her, she remembers an appointment.

Remember, when dealing with a Shadow:

DO

- Let them know that you are not interested in oblique comments by either ignoring them or pinning them down to facts

- Ask precise questions to clarify and simplify what they are saying then offer a reduced list of possibilities or courses of action
- Clearly define Shadows' boundaries, telling them that it will simplify things for them if they stay within these boundaries
- Provide support where appropriate but without compromising yourself. These people are usually very capable when they have to be
- Before finishing your conversation, check if there is 'any other business'. Shadows have a wonderful way of pulling things out of a hat later on and saying, 'You never asked'
- Check back regularly, maintaining any authority you have and giving any support you can
- Remember that Shadows can quickly become over-familiar if encouraged too far. This is because it strengthens their feeling of being special.

DON'T

- Join in the intrigue or appear to enjoy the innuendo
- Reinforce their vagueness by accepting over-complicated situations, long, rambling stories or explanations
- Leave loose ends. They could tie you up in knots later on.

How to deal effectively with a Shadow

SHELLEY: Hey Jane! Have you got a moment?
JANE: Hello there, I wanted to see you. How are things going?
SHELLEY: Well, the same as usual, I suppose. Have you heard about Mr Rowe's problem?
JANE: If Mr Rowe has a problem I'm sure he'll come and tell me about it himself. Now, I asked for some information from you.

SHELLEY: Oh, but it's not just him. Janice in Radiography hasn't been able to get any work done for almost two weeks.

JANE: I spoke with Janice this morning and it appears there are no problems in Radiography. What I am more interested in from you is that information I asked for. When can I have it?

SHELLEY: Oh, I've hardly had time with all these disturbances.

JANE: How have these 'disturbances' affected your work?

SHELLEY: Well, I've been trying to help Mr Rowe sort his problems out and then there was Ethel...

JANE: If you have a specific problem relating your work then please come and tell me and we can try and sort something out.

SHELLEY: I can do my work OK, it's just with all these interruptions...

JANE: Don't feel you have to be there to sort other people's problems out. You are only required to carry out the tasks you've been given. Do as described in your job description. And at the moment I am most interested in seeing the information I asked for a week ago.

SHELLEY: [looking hurt] Are you saying that I don't know how to do my job?

JANE: I'm saying that you are an important part of the team, too important to let yourself be distracted by details which aren't part of your job. I really need that information and you are the person I count on to get it for me. Please focus on that.

SHELLEY: Well, don't blame me if things get worse around here...

JANE: How soon can I have that information?

SHELLEY: I'll get on with it now. If I don't get interrupted you'll have it in the morning. But I mean, no interruptions, I can't do six things at once.

JANE: Thanks.

Putting the strategy into action

The key when trying to circumvent or prevent Shadow behaviour is to remain specific and focused on the job in hand (or the job you would like them to get on with). In extreme cases they will have many different ways for changing the subject. Tantalising gossip, innuendo and knowing but vague remarks are all designed to throw us off-course or prevent us insisting on something we would like them to do. They may also step up their tactics with a display of tears, mock indignation, sulks or vague threats ('You mark my words, it'll end badly'), as they feel that their exit routes are blocked off one by one. If pushed too far or handled clumsily, Shadows may resort to sudden unexplained absences or complaints about someone else's harassing or bullying tactics.

The idea behind the strategy above is to help Shadows focus and support them as they get on with their work. Keep the message simple, polite and firm, and avoid getting drawn into irrelevant debates. Keep discussions short and to the point, but remain attentive and supportive. Once you have agreement on a specific course of action, check back with them regularly in a supportive way.

Finally, before leaving them to get on with something, ask them, 'What could go wrong?' The aim here is to get them to think ahead and spot any appointments or distractions they may have 'forgotten' when agreeing to arrangements with you. This will help prevent the 'Didn't I tell you? I always finish early on a Thursday' type of excuse for not finishing what was asked of them.

THE SILENT TYPE

These are unresponsive people who either give the impression that they are immensely intelligent or very stupid, though of course they are neither. Nevertheless, spending time with a Silent Type can be both frustrating and uncomfortable. They frequently try our patience as conversation seems to be virtually impossible for them and getting anything started takes special skills.

Their lack of conversation, the silences, grunts and minimal responses all conspire to make communications between us worse. Typically, when faced with someone who does not seem to want to respond we tend to step up our efforts to encourage interaction. This is the last thing we should be doing with a Silent Type, because unless we are careful, we wind up having the conversation for them or stringing multiple questions together that would be difficult to answer even by someone who was in a more balanced conversation with us.

The route to take with the Silent Type is first to calm our own need for a reply. We have to be comfortable with the silences, otherwise we will be tempted to fill the gaps ourselves. The other person can't answer if we are talking all the time.

The second point is to use 'open questions'. These tend to require some sort of narrative as a response by using a *how, what, when, where* or *who* opener. (In contrast 'closed' questions which can be answered with a simple "Yes" or "No" tend to discourage conversation.)

It is common to interpret the long silences as insolent or uncooperative behaviour. Such interpretations are unhelpful and there are a number of other possibilities that we should keep in mind. For example, a Silent Type may be uncomfortable with the situation or the surroundings; they may not be gifted conversationalists or they may lack the necessary social skills; they may not understand our questions or the purpose of the discussion; they may be stressed, uncomfortable or afraid.

Typical Silent Type characteristics

- They respond minimally without committing themselves, with answers like 'Yes', 'No', 'I suppose so'

- Their silence can give the impression they know something and are biding their time, that they are mulling over what has been said, or that they are above the tedious reality of routine
- We tend to start (mis)interpreting their behaviour as insolent or uncooperative.

The Silent Type in action

Scene: Aldo knocks on the door of his manager Karen's office

KAREN: Hi there! Thanks for coming to see me – there were a couple of matters I wanted to chat with you about. It seems you have had some problems lately, is that true?

ALDO: [silence]

KAREN: I understand that things haven't been going so well in your department lately. I've been told that our normal response time for client queries has gone up from seven days to four weeks! What have you got to say for yourself? It is your responsibility after all, isn't it?

ALDO: [silence]

KAREN: It's not good enough. If you have problems coping then you should come and see me immediately and we'll see what we can do about it. Do you understand?

ALDO: [long pause] Yes.

KAREN: So what's been going on?

ALDO: [silence]

KAREN: Are things going to improve in the future?

ALDO: [nods]

KAREN: Okay then, I don't want to hear any more complaints about your department. Agreed?

ALDO: [shrugs]

KAREN: Is there anything else you wanted to 'say'?

ALDO: Is that all?

KAREN: If there's nothing else, but keep me informed...

What went wrong?

Karen responded exactly as most of us do. Faced with Aldo's unresponsiveness she starts to speak more quickly rather than slowing the pace down. This makes her seem more threatening and impatient and puts extra pressure on Aldo. Not a good strategy. She would be better advised to prepare for the meeting by making sure she is calm and has sufficient time to devote to it. It would also be useful to make sure that the environment is not too threatening; many people regard being called to their manager's office as stressful or suspicious, and may find it hard to relax and speak naturally.

Karen could also start up the conversation with some sort of 'ice-breaker' or informal chat to put Aldo at his ease. I know that some people regard this tactic with suspicion, especially when they are not use to it. As long as it is sincere and used appropriately, however, it is likely to create a more relaxed atmosphere. Remember, too, that the right sort of questions (interested, open-ended ones) will engage the Silent Type mentally in the process. The question 'What do you like about living here?' requires the listener to construct a response. This has a significantly different effect from the kind of demand a closed-ended question makes of them, such as 'Do you live here?' This only needs a 'yes' or 'no' answer and is usually quickly followed up with another similar question, which can start to feel more like an interrogation.

Remember, when dealing with a Silent Type:

DO

- Put them at their ease with small talk before tackling the main issues
- Ask open-ended questions
- Maintain open and expectant body language

- If no reply is forthcoming, gently question their lack of response
- Avoid putting them under too much pressure
- Tell them what you expect and make simple demands rather than long, convoluted and detailed explanations
- Give them time to think about it
- If you plan another meeting, write down what you expect
- End the interaction yourself, in a friendly way, and let them know you are looking forward to your next meeting.

DON'T

- Make conversation for them. If they stop speaking, wait, be comfortable with the silence
- Talk too much or cut them off. When they do start speaking, remember it's like starting a car on a cold morning, let it run for a few minutes
- Let the meeting stumble to a close. Finish it yourself in a neat and tidy way with a brief list of your requirements or a summary of the discussion.

How to deal effectively with a Silent Type

KAREN: Hi there! Thanks for coming to see me, take a seat. Can I get you something, tea, coffee?
ALDO: Er, no thanks.
KAREN: You are just back from holiday, aren't you, where did you go?
ALDO: [pause] We went to Spain, near Malaga. We go there most years.
KAREN: You must like it then. What do you like most about it?
ALDO: Well, you feel more at home in a place you know, and the facilities are brilliant, specially the sporting activities.

KAREN: Hmm, I'll remember that when I'm booking my holiday next year, I always prefer to go on a recommendation. By the way, Aldo, I've been wanting to thank you for coping with the changes in your department over the last few months. How have you been managing?

ALDO: [pause] OK.

KAREN: It's just that I've noticed a bit of a backlog in dealing with some client enquiries. Is there any particular reason for that?

ALDO: [silence]

KAREN: We used to respond to all enquiries within seven days, it seems that some are waiting as long as a month now. Why is that?

ALDO: [silence]

KAREN: [after about ten seconds and taking care not to sound too demanding] Aldo, I asked you a question. Can you suggest any reason for that?

ALDO: [long pause] We used to have eleven people in my group, we only have three since levels were cut.

KAREN: I see, understandably there has been an effect then. Do you have any thoughts on how things could be improved?

ALDO: [silence]

KAREN: Aldo, I'd really like your ideas, no one knows your department better than you do. Perhaps you have some idea on how we could work round the staffing problem?

ALDO: [pause] I have been thinking about that. Maybe we could start a two-tier system so we deal with all urgent enquiries first.

KAREN: That sounds like a good idea. Tell you what, make a note of how it would work – keep to the main points – and we can discuss it tomorrow before I go to the management meeting.

ALDO: OK.

KAREN: Is two o'clock tomorrow OK, right after lunch?

ALDO: Uh huh.

KAREN: [standing up] See you then, thanks for coming to see me, and I'm really pleased we are working things out.

Putting the strategy into action

The main asset in handling this sort of silent and unresponsive behaviour productively is our own creativity. When we run out of ideas we tend to dry up or slip back into 'interrogation' mode. If you know you have to deal with someone like this on a regular basis then it is worth planning and trying out various creative approaches, openers and questions to see what sort of response you get. As a working hypothesis, consider that the Silent Type is likely to be internally focused (on what is going on inside them) and may be mentally engaging very little with the outside world, ourselves included, so the first step is to draw them out in some way. This can take time and so it may be appropriate to set a little time aside to build a relationship by doing things that don't relate directly to the questions you need to discuss with them. In the workplace this may be as simple as a manager becoming more 'visible' on a regular basis so that the more formal meetings are more comfortable.

As for the discussion outlined above, setting the scene is important and the rule is, 'first the relationship, then the response'. Karen starts out to put Aldo at his ease. This rapport-building stage is essential if the meeting is to have any chance of success. She starts by thanking him for coming to see her (consider a handshake in greeting if appropriate) and goes through the usual courtesies before quite naturally turning the conversation to (in this case) Aldo's holiday. She is careful to monitor her delivery and gently prompts him when the silence lasts too long.

As far as possible she allows him to set the pace of the conversation and her requests for information are simple and few.

She ends the meeting decisively, though not abruptly, since prolonging it will only put Aldo under more pressure. This not only means that she is in control of the discussion, choosing to end it before they get into another 'stalemate' situation, it also tells Aldo that future meetings might not be too bad.

THE GROUSER

Grousers are eternally negative. Their behaviour seems to start from the point of view that, in any event, things can only go wrong or get worse. Their immediate and automatic response in any situation is to highlight the problems, and if there aren't any, to comment on the downside. When others are trying to solve difficulties or improve a procedure, Grousers cast a negative pall over everything. Perhaps they don't intentionally start out to throw a wet blanket over any idea; maybe they just feel unable to change things because they have never learned what it is to have power or to be in control of their own destiny. Or their constant negativity may be an insurance against disappointment. Whatever lies behind the behaviour, Grousers are never prepared to raise their sights or to see things in a more optimistic light. Unfortunately, they can quickly bring down the people around them as well. Having to deal with this difficult behaviour can be frustrating and tiring, but there are ways of getting around it.

Before we move on to the strategy though, a word about depression. The thinking styles used by Grousers are very similar to the way people view the world when they are depressed. This does not necessarily mean that if you are working with a Grouser they are depressed, but if you have noticed a significant worsening of their behaviour this may indicate something more than a pessimistic outlook. In the workplace, it may signal an occupational health issue rather than simply a matter of difficult behaviour.

Another proviso in dealing with a Grouser is that they may have a point. Their behaviour may seem to be saying 'Just go away and leave me alone' and that is what, in the end, many of us would do when faced with such insistent unhelpfulness. But their negative world view might contain useful information about what could go wrong and in some situations we might be able to use that.

Or their negativity may be a reflection of how they feel about their job; they may need help in their work or perhaps something has happened which has led to them feeling left out, demotivated or hopeless. Maybe they cannot see their way to avoid a problem, or don't have the thinking skills in a given situation to navigate their way through a challenge. Then it becomes all the more necessary to help them break the task down, identifying any obstacles they envisage in a concrete way, so problems can be resolved or avoided rather than used as a reason for not advancing.

Typical Grouser characteristics

- They meet positive suggestions with comments like, 'It won't work', 'It's impossible' or 'We've already tried that'
- They are eternal pessimists. If it is raining, they complain. On a sunny day, they tell you it's too hot and that the garden needs rain
- They can bring down those around them because they can be so hard to deal with
- They do not respond to the positive statements we may use to try to counter their negativity.

The Grouser in action

Scene: Michael is trying to get Anne to circulate some information

MICHAEL: Hi Anne, how're things?

ANNE: How do you think? Six weeks I've been putting up with the most impossible conditions, cramped in this tiny office. I'm sure it's against regulations – aren't we supposed to have so many square feet or something?

MICHAEL: You don't know how lucky you are! Look at the nice view you've got from your window there.

ANNE: View? Fat lot of good that is, I never get time to look at it, even if I could, twisting round in my chair to see I'd probably do myself an injury.

MICHAEL: You could turn your desk round a bit then you'd be able to work and look out of the window.

ANNE: I haven't got time for all that. What did you want me for anyway?

MICHAEL: Well, you know that we are having a meeting of the whole department tomorrow afternoon, I'd like you to call all the supervisors and politely remind them to be on time.

ANNE: Call who? Do you know how many there are? Besides, all grade two supervisors will be tied up today so I won't be able to reach them.

MICHAEL: [floundering] Do your best, and I'll check back later.

ANNE: Don't bother. I've told you, it can't be done – we've had terrible trouble with this telephone system lately – so even if I can get through, most of them won't be there anyway. You'd do better to cancel the meeting.

What went wrong?

Every comment Michael makes is met with Anne's all-consuming sense of hopelessness. His natural response is to try to reframe her negative comments with a few positive ones of his own. Unfortunately, to a Grouser, this simply confirms that we have not heard them so they step up their attempts to prove how hopeless things are. The first rule here is to let the Grouser know that you are not challenging their view of things by saying something that acknowledges it – that you have heard their point of view without sharing it. It goes something like this:

Me: Hi, David. Lovely weather, isn't it?

Grouser: OK if you can stand the heat, it's too hot to get any work done.

Me: Yes, I know it can be hard working in conditions like this.

David will probably not be satisfied to leave it there. He would probably add something like:

'Hard? It's impossible. I don't know why we put up with it, I really don't.'

To which I would respond with something like 'Hmmm', before leading the conversation towards the subject I wanted to discuss with David:

'When would be a good time to discuss this new allocation system we are introducing?'

It is useful when dealing with negative behaviour like this to stick to facts, rather than opinions, and to stay out of any sort of debate that allows the other person to respond with a negative statement. Even so, some people can manage to put a downbeat interpretation on anything. The idea is to acknowledge that you have heard them and move on.

As well as the overriding negativity, another conspicuous feature of the Grouser's style of delivery is their habit of lumping everything together by making general statements including words like 'always', 'never' and 'everyone'; for example, 'Everyone knows...' or 'We never get a moment's peace around here'. This global thinking style, as it is known, leads the person to make non-specific statements about the general and all-pervasive nature of their negative experience. Thus '*All* managers/men/women are bad news', or '*Nothing* ever works out for me'. It would be hard work to challenge every one of these statements and anyway, the Grouser probably wouldn't take them on board. Such globalised statements do need to be tackled, though, by concentrating on specifics. An example of this came from a teenage boy I heard responding to his mother's accusation that he was 'always getting into trouble at school'. (She was not a Grouser, by the way, just a normal mother responding to a normal 14-year-old.) His commendable reply was a polite 'When *specifically* was I in trouble the last time?' This direct question got his mother to focus on specific information, gently challenging the global use of *always*. The conversation quickly became more productive.

I suggest that in dealing with the Grouser's invasive habit of globalising, you ask them to support only the statements that actually matter in the situation. So, for example, it is not worth challenging negative comments about the weather, but it would be a good idea to point out that some managers are reliable and supportive.

Finally, remember that it is a Grouser's world view that we are dealing with here; to them it may appear that we want to challenge their *beliefs* about love, life and the meaning of everything. Before tackling the Grouser head-on, think about how you took it when someone tried to change your beliefs. Most of us become even more dogmatic when someone tries to tell us we are wrong. Only tackle the important issues with a Grouser, and then do it thoughtfully.

Remember, when dealing with a Grouser:

DO

- Stay out of their negative spiral
- Reframe their negative interpretations
- Acknowledge their complaints and feelings, but don't agree, then add your own positive tag statements at the end, eg acknowledge that it's raining and say that you are looking forward to a time when the fine weather comes back
- Always use 'and' to link your positive statement to theirs. If you use 'but' it sounds like a challenge
- Acknowledge their insight into the difficulties, then ask what might be done in a factual, problem-solving way – keep it theoretical with questions like 'In an ideal world, with your instinct for these things, what do you think might be done...?'
- Thank them for their observations, but let them know that you will be going ahead anyway. In other words, you are accepting what they say, but not the belief behind it

- Identify from what they say if there are any real obstacles that may need to be foreseen.

DON'T

- Openly challenge their negative statements. Remember they need it, and besides, it has been said of the Grouser that if you tell them that every cloud has a silver lining they'll just point out to you that the silver lining could drop out any moment and kill somebody
- Try and cheer them up
- Reinforce their negativity by agreeing with it.

How to deal effectively with a Grouser

MICHAEL: Hi Anne, how're things?

ANNE: How do you think? Six weeks I've been putting up with the most impossible conditions cramped in this tiny office. I'm sure it's against regulations – aren't we supposed to have so many square feet or something?

MICHAEL: I know it's not very big. The advantage is that you can reach everything from where you are sitting. Now, Anne, you know that we are having a meeting of the whole department tomorrow afternoon, I'd like you to call all the supervisors and politely remind them to be on time.

ANNE: Call who? Do you know how many there are? Besides, all grade two supervisors will be tied up today so I won't be able to reach them.

MICHAEL: There are 13 of them. It may take a couple of hours but I know how thorough you are and that you'll do it properly.

ANNE: Don't count on it. We've had terrible trouble with this telephone system lately – and even if I can get through, most of them won't be there anyway, it's Thursday!

MICHAEL: You've been having trouble, have you? Keep a note if you have any problems with the phone, and I'll get it checked out. Now, anything more you need from me to get the job done?

ANNE: I won't be able to reach all of them, what do I do about that?

MICHAEL: If you can't manage to contact any of them, let me know and I'll handle it myself. Thanks for pointing it out; I didn't know it could be so difficult. Keep a note of the times you call and the number of calls you make. It could be that I need to have a word with them about their availability in future, but I'll need facts.

Putting the strategy into action

Straight away Michael's responds to Anne's version of reality by acknowledging her comment about the size of her office. He then adds a positive tag (a positive comment 'The advantage is...' linked to the truism 'I know it's not very big'). The idea of this tag is to let the other person know that, although you accept their view of the world, there may be other interpretations – you accept what they say but do not share their pessimistic view.

Michael gently and persistently challenges Anne's negativity with specific responses, but only where he thought it was relevant. So to her statement 'Do you know how many there are?', he replied by giving the actual number of supervisors. It is much easier dealing with an exact number than something non-specific.

He wanted to avoid being drawn in by vague comments or innuendo, so he did not bother to respond to her remark about the significance of Thursday. On the other hand, he acknowledged the factual information such as the unavailability of the supervisors and trouble with the telephone system. He went further by asking her to record how often she called; this is encouraging her to think factually about the difficulties she is having so that she can report back concrete information on which Michael can act. He did the same regarding the telephone problems. He wants her to understand that if she converts the 'terrible trouble' into something more definite, others can then act on it.

The message is: 'I acknowledge your point of view, but I am going ahead anyway'. This is best delivered in a helpful and supportive manner. And for the Grouser to feel understood, it helps to acknowledge what they are saying before moving on. Some of their negativity will doubtless be based on fact.

Chapter 10
Looking for new ideas

When considering approaches to dealing with a difficult relationship it is useful to stand back and look at the *patterns* of behaviour of those involved, rather than becoming engrossed in who-said-what-to-whom. It can be tough to remain objective when we believe that someone is treating us unjustly or disrespectfully, and it can seem unfair that we have to make an effort because they seem unable or unwilling to. Even so it will be worth the effort. The central problem is often not the interaction itself, but how we view it - not in our actions but in our thinking.

When we start changing our thinking, we have a wider choice of actions open to us. Over the years, thanks to the many people I have met in the course of my work, I have developed a number of memory joggers to help avoid a difficult situation becoming worse. The ideas listed in this chapter can provide, I hope, new insights into how you might navigate a troublesome relationship.

The ASSUME technique

Most of us act spontaneously, in a pre-programmed way, when we are confronted by difficult behaviour. We frequently get stuck like a needle in a groove, reacting the same way every time somebody is being difficult. It is therefore very important to adopt a technique that allows us to see what is really going on. Regardless of the circumstances, the person or the people you are confronted by, this is the 'stop, look and listen' approach to problem-solving in challenging situations. I call it the ASSUME technique because it will allow you to assume an active position of control and set you up for success. The technique enables you to step back and check your own behaviour while simultaneously gathering information. It will allow you to remain in control, to maintain your objectivity and to be more aware of where you are in an interaction.

Next time you come up against a difficult person (or beforehand, if you have the chance) think of the word ASSUME. It will guide you through six simple steps to help you respond.

Assess the situation

Identify what is actually happening. What are the behaviour or actions that contribute to the difficulty? What is the dispute about? Is it entirely the other person's fault that there is a problem, or do you too have some responsibility for the difficulties? Perhaps your adversary makes a habit of being a difficult person. Check around. Is he or she difficult with everybody in the same way, or is there something about your behaviour that is unwittingly contributing to the difficult situation? Avoid 'he-said-she-said' analysis and stick to observable facts.

Stop wishing the difficult person were different

It is amazing how much energy we waste, waiting for somebody to change, hoping for a miracle cure. It is unlikely that the person will change, so you need to actively *do* something. This step makes it possible. Accept the person for what they are, that they are manifesting difficult behaviour for whatever reason and move on to the next stage.

Step back

In order to respond constructively to the problem, you must look at the difficult behaviour from an objective standpoint. By seeing it as a whole you will be able to notice the key points in that person's behaviour that could reveal the pattern of behaviour you are dealing with. Ask yourself, 'Have I ever acted that way?' Perhaps you can identify with their conduct, which could give useful clues about their needs or how to tackle the behaviour. In any case, the ability to step back gives us the space to ask ourselves 'What do I want to happen here?'

Understand your strategy

Once you have identified the type of difficult behaviour you are dealing with you will have a pretty good idea of how the person will react in certain situations. Then you can put together your plan of action. Take time to think each step through, and try to anticipate all possible outcomes. Write the plan down if necessary and memorise or rehearse it. It will pay dividends. When you purposely choose a course of action it puts you in control. Only by remaining in control can you master the situation.

Master the situation

Objectively assessing the situation allows you to master it because you are deliberately deciding on each step you take. This does not mean 'winning', rather that our actions are part of a planned approach. It may even mean that we choose *not* to persist with a particular tack because we consider the cost is too high (remember the three Cs). Choice puts us in control, so choose your moment and the appropriate course of action. For example, if your plan calls for being alone with the person, make sure you will not be interrupted; if it calls for a little time to build a better relationship, consider changing the setting. Use the strategies that are demonstrated in this book to nip that difficult behaviour in the bud.

Expect to have to do it again

With most types of difficult people you can expect, at some time or another, to have to remind them firmly that you will not accept their bad behaviour. This should not be done in an 'I've told you before...', accusing sort of way. Simply repeat the strategy that worked the first time. If you work with the public, you are more likely to have a regular turnover of difficult people. How can you refine your skills to be more effective next time? Look at the results of your action. Ask yourself if it can be improved. Keep your strategy handy and be ready to use it on another occasion.

Remember to stand back and look for patterns in the behaviour. Use the ASSUME technique, rather than getting emotionally caught up in the details. Formulate your strategy then tackle that behaviour confidently.

The SALVAGE strategy

Sometimes a difficult situation goes past the point where the ASSUME technique can be used. Angry people are on auto-pilot, so I would recommend using the SALVAGE strategy to defuse, rather than escalate, the situation. This provides useful steps to follow in any situation marked by tension. At its core the SALVAGE strategy is intended to be a non-threatening platform on which to build more constructive communications.

Smile

It is wonderful how disarming a congenial, non-threatening approach can be. Take the initiative, step forward with a smile, a handshake or some other sign of how affable you are. Of course, there are some situations where smiling would be inappropriate. Nevertheless, you should be pro-active - your conduct and gestures aiming to demonstrate that you are not 'the enemy'.

Anticipate their anger

If you are dealing with a hostile or angry person then you know they are likely to act in a hostile or angry way. Are you a duck or a sponge? Do their hostile insults run off your back or do you soak them up? Accept the anger as 'information' about how they feel rather than an attack on you personally (even though they may attempt to make it personal). Remember Eleanor Roosevelt's words: 'No one can make you feel inferior without your consent.'

Listen to them

Listen non-defensively. Consider listening as a holistic exercise in communication. 'Seek first to understand' is the motto here. What is driving them? What do they need to help them calm down? (Which may not be the same as whatever they are asking for). Have you understood? Ask relevant questions to find out what they want or what the complaint is about.

Verify that you have understood

Summarise your understanding of their points. Do not attempt to challenge, contradict or correct them. Simply confirm your understanding. Open with a phrase along the lines of 'Just to make sure I have understood...' before enumerating their points. Stick to observable facts in your summary. Leave out their subjective interpretations, insults or jibes.

Attend to their needs

Apart from the demands they are making, do they have any

other immediate needs that could be satisfied? Are they comfortable, do they know how long they will have to wait? If a long wait is involved, could they go away and come back? Are they uncertain about anything - a procedure or how the system works? Maybe all they need is an acknowledgement - 'I am sorry you have been caused all this trouble' is an expression of regret, not an admission of liability. A sincere comment like this can work wonders.

Guarantee something will be done

Tell them what you are going to do and do it. Let them know how long it will take and any other relevant information. If you need 10 minutes to check on something, come back to them in nine with the response. (If you haven't got the response in 10 minutes, keep them informed anyway.)

Remember that angry or stressed people don't hear fine detail, so stick to the main points and avoid negatives and loaded words ('I am here to help you sort this out' rather than 'I *don't want* you to be *disappointed*').

If there is nothing you can do then you have to say so, but do it in a way that sounds as if you are doing something. Offer a list of alternatives rather than a flat 'no'.

Encourage them to change direction

Finally, and having got this far with the process, encourage the person on some course of action other than complaining. It might be anything from giving them a newspaper to read, referring them to another service, or persuading them to call back another day. Having built a little rapport it is useful to try and influence their behaviour in some way.

I designed the ASSUME technique to help prepare for tricky situations and the SALVAGE strategy for responding to irate or demanding people. Both can be used either face-to-face or on the telephone. These simple bullet-pointed approaches are intended as reminders of how to act, rather than prescriptions. You already have your own strategies or skills that work for you. The suggestions above are intended as additions, to provide a fresh way of thinking about how you approach tricky or demanding situations. They will not cover every eventuality you may encounter, and the choice of words you use must be yours, rather than a script provided by me. Where I have suggested phrases these are intended as illustrations. If you regularly face a particular type of situation – say, you have to calm angry people on the telephone or give out bad news such as refusal of a service on a regular basis – then it is worth taking the time to plan your response based on the principles I am describing here.

I recommend that individuals or teams come up with the sort of response that is 'right' for their situation. Getting the team to brainstorm and plan can also reveal some hidden talents and surprisingly good ideas. Once you have planned the steps you can agree the form of words to be used. I am against scripts, but once everyone in the team knows the 'approved' way of responding they can adapt it using their own words. This can also give a boost to their confidence.

Separating impact from intent

I call this the three Is for simplicity: *Insight, Impact* and *Intent*. Take a situation you are not happy with involving another person and ask yourself the three questions overleaf. If you are in the position of managing others or mediating between protagonists in difficult situations, you will find this an invaluable first step in disentangling facts from emotions. The process requires that you stick to observable behaviour and exclude any conjecture or speculation as to possible motive or intentions.

Insight - What did they actually do?

Start by identifying the actions that have led to the problem. To do this you have to be objective, taking the role of witness rather than participant. So, rather than saying: 'John came straight in and without any warning just laid into me with all sorts of unjustified attacks...', you could say: 'John walked in and shouted at me'.

Impact - How did this really affect me?

Honestly review your feelings and the effect of the other person's behaviour, eg: 'When John shouted my heartbeat went up and my legs felt weak. I felt insulted and angry. I wanted to shout back'.

Intent - What assumptions am I making?

As long as the other person's intention remains obscure we are likely to fill in the gaps in our understanding with assumptions about their motives. These are usually wrong. All we can really know are the answers to the two questions above. We can only discover John's intentions by asking him about them.

In dealing with a difficult person, don't be afraid to ask about their intentions. If necessary, explain the impact on you with something like, 'When you shouted I wanted to get angry' or 'When you came in you seemed (to me) angry and that upset me'.

The DAB response

An alternative way of handling such a situation is to use the DAB response.

'When you (Do what you do)...' – explain the incident or difficult behaviour objectively. Stick to the observable facts about what actually happened.

'I feel (it has **A**ffected me)...' – tell the person about your feelings, making sure you frame it in the first person. Using 'I' demonstrates that you accept and take responsibility for your feelings ('I feel bad', rather than 'You make me feel bad').

'I feel like this (**B**ecause)...' – this is an extension of the first person self-assertive approach above. Statements like 'I feel bad because I don't handle shouting very well' or 'I feel bad because I thought you were attacking me' explain the process that was happening in you. This helps remind the other individual that you, too, are a person with feelings.

Help it flow

Another useful checklist to remember is Enquire, Summarise and Acknowledge.

Enquire about what the person wants to achieve. Remember the maxim 'Seek first to understand' and always be sure to avoid the statement disguised as question, for example, 'Are you daft?' when you really mean 'I think you are daft', or 'How do you expect me to answer that?' when you really want to say 'I can't answer that.'

Summarise your understanding of the situation. This allows you to show that you have heard and also to check you have grasped what they are trying to convey.

Acknowledge their contribution. This will indicate that you validate (not necessarily agree with) their point of view and tells them that you accept what is real for them.

Moving your goat

Sometimes people are quite simply intent on riling us; on getting our goat. A wise goatherd once said: 'In order to get your goat they've got to know where your goat is tied up. I keep moving mine'. If you don't want them to get your goat, don't let them know where it is. The seven steps to remaining in control are as follows:

Say you are sorry, and mean it

We often use 'sorry' as a verbal tic. How often have you said the word over the last two weeks when you didn't need to or without really meaning it? By contrast, how often have you not said it when it was warranted and would really have helped? A sincere expression of regret can work wonders. Saying sorry does not imply that you take the blame for anything that has occurred. 'I am sorry that this has happened to you', or 'I am sorry we argued' do not automatically mean 'I know it is all my fault and I am giving in to you and you are winning and I have lost and all that other stuff'.

Breathe from the diaphragm

Take a deep breath, hold your tongue (try sitting on your hands), and pay attention to what the other person is saying.

Listen, listen and listen again

Seek first to understand, no need to say more. Ask open questions to clarify but be very careful not to interrogate or fire off questions defensively.

Moderate your voice

We are often unaware of how much we raise our voice when we are becoming distressed. It sounds louder to the other person than it does to us and this will start to crank up the argument or simply shut the other person down.

Acknowledge your feelings

First identify and acknowledge your feelings to yourself. Then explain how you feel to the other person, using 'I' statements (see the DAB response above).

Take a break

It takes two to start an argument but only one to stop it. If you do decide to break off the discussion to collect your thoughts or allow time for calming down, first tell the other person with a line like 'I need a little time to think about this', or 'I'll be back when I'm more able to concentrate'. If they insist that you continue, stay firm. Simply repeat the explanation linked to your intention to continue at a later time.

Find out what is important to them

What is it they really need you, or someone else, to hear? A simple question like 'I was wondering what the most important points are to you?', or 'I'm really interested to know how you feel about it' shows interest and favours a collaboration over confrontation.

You can also use humour, but tread carefully. Humour can work wonders as long as it is spontaneous and natural but can be disastrous if it feels in any way set up or contrived. If in doubt leave it out, especially if your difficult person is already using it (see dealing with a Guerrilla on page 135).

Handling criticism

Generally speaking, I adopt the attitude that complaints are valid, criticism is not. The distinction here is that a complaint is an account given by one person to another about something which is inconvenient, inappropriate, obstructive or whatever. Criticism does the same, but the critic adds a personal attack to the complaint. This is highly damaging because – apart from the potential for emotional upset or even psychological harm in extreme cases – criticising can also ruin relationships. At the very least it leads to ruffled feathers, as the target of the criticism hears the personal attack rather than the complaint. When we feel criticised we are more likely to respond to the attack than the complaint, because quite rightly we feel as if we have been verbally set upon. Even if the complaint is perfectly valid we are more likely to reject it if we don't like the wrapping.

The way to take control of a critical attack is to change our response so that the force of the criticism is diluted. Paradoxically, criticism thrives on resistance; every force exerts an equal and opposite force. The two opposing forces act in a reciprocal way, each feeding off the other in an almost endless spiral of escalation. I push you and you push me back in some way. But what happens if I take away the resistance?

I am not suggesting that we ignore criticism – though that is not bad advice at times – I am proposing that we subdue the attack with a constructive response.

Basically, you have three possible courses of action in the face of criticism:

1. You can react with a counter-attack, which is likely to make things worse. Psychologist John Gottman calls this 'cross complaining' and it is a standard approach many of us adopt when we feel attacked. As Gottman says: 'This pattern will continue until one or both (participants) decide to focus on one complaint at a time and try to understand each other's point of view.'[1]

2. You can ignore the criticism. This will not make it go away but if you can stay out of the critical/defensive spiral you may be able to avoid having your day ruined. Ignoring criticism is especially important when it is 'meant well'. This is sometimes called 'constructive criticism'. After all, for what reason would someone who genuinely means us no harm want to criticise us? Possibly they have their own agenda, or perhaps they feel angry about something else they don't know how to tell us. You will need to listen out for this – see the next point.

3. You can listen carefully and respond as outlined below. It may seem counter-intuitive to listen and act constructively rather than respond with criticisms of our own or

rationalise our behaviour, but it is worth the effort. Here is how:

1. Ask questions and do not give explanations

Listen to the complaint, ignoring any insults, judgements, globalisations ('you never do this', or 'you are always doing that', and so on), exaggerations or inaccuracies.

2. Acknowledge what you have heard without judging

Let the speaker know that you have heard what they have said, avoid retaliation, self-justification or a need to explain the whys and wherefores.

3. Avoid getting drawn into a debate at this stage

To avoid the situation escalating into an argument, keep your response to a minimum, even if you are smarting from what you perceive as an attack.

4. Make allowances for the other person

When people are stressed, worried, depressed, overworked or tired, they are never at their best and things are likely to get out of proportion (and out of control).

5. De-personalise the criticism

Treat criticism as information about how the other person sees the situation, rather than an attack on you.

6. Consider that the speaker takes the points seriously

Use the noise level and vehemence of the attack to gauge how seriously the other person needs to get their point across. Anger may indicate frustration at not being heard. If the criticism is coming from your spouse or partner, recall the words of one distinguished couples therapist[2] who said: 'It just is not that personal an insult to be criticised by a distressed spouse'.

7. Break off the interaction

Move away, end the interview, take a break, change the subject to something more agreeable (make sure that you acknowledge what you have heard first).

8. Take heed and change

The most powerful strategy is to change the situation so that the criticism is no longer valid. The ability to want to learn from such interactions and to change the situation for the better as a result is a personal triumph, not a failure. Only use this if it is appropriate. If you judge that the other person has a point, however badly put, and you are able to overlook the criticism and respond to the underlying complaint this is fine. We all need to compromise sometimes. However, if you think you are constantly doing this to keep the peace or appease the other person, beware! This would be like throwing steaks to a tiger in the hope that it will become a vegetarian.

Stepping stones to solutions

The ultimate aim of any intervention described in this book is to make working or living with difficult people more bearable. As I have said before, we may not be able to change them but we can change how we work with them. One of the perennial difficulties in working with difficult relationships is that the antagonism felt by the participants acts as a wedge which keeps them apart. This makes any attempts at repair difficult since, understandably, they are not generally eager to engage in the process. This is where one of the basic maxims of change comes into its own.

If it is not working, do something different

Think about any protracted argument or dispute. The chances are that the original reason for the dispute has long since been buried under the hurt and disrespect that the two sides have heaped on each other in their failed attempts to resolve it. In this process, the more time passes the greater the despondency and hopelessness at ever finding an equitable solution. Ask either side what they think of their chances, or the other side, and you'll get an answer loaded with pessimism and accusations.

But no situation is totally hopeless. There are always some aspects that are working, times when it did work or moments when the dispute is less disruptive and both sides call a momentary truce or are able to co-exist. What is needed is a way of breaking the cycle of blame and working towards a solution.

Distinguish blame from contribution

Authors Stone, Patton and Heen of the Harvard Negotiation Project say: 'At heart, blame is about judging and contribution is about understanding'.[3] Blame may be the appropriate course of action to take sometimes, that is not at issue here. If the name of the game is to work with a difficult person, however, to move forward and get results, blame will be counter-productive. When blame is implied or intended the likely result is a reaction: defensiveness, raised emotions, arguments and interruptions.

Discussing contribution raises a different range of responses. Questions to ask are 'How did each of us contribute to this situation?' or better still 'Given that we have both contributed to this, how can we both act to get ourselves out of it?' The people involved can then start to write a prescription for action. Understanding contribution is useful when we need to recognise how to change things for the better and so avoid a similar problem in the future.

Encouraging collaboration

The next step is to encourage a collaborative stance in order to move forward. This can take a little time and may not be done at a single meeting. However, it is never too early to start talking about how 'we' are going to work together on the things 'we' want to improve.

One idea I have found very useful is to target the relationship rather than the individuals. This is relatively easy to do following some sort of crisis. Say, for example, that a colleague has been given a rough ride by another, that both have been under pressure because of changes at work, that their relationship has been deteriorating as a result and is now at a stand-off with them barely speaking. Rather than targeting their behaviour, I point out that they have both been through a hard time because of external pressures, that these pressures would have made near-impossible demands on any relationship because, for example, of conflicting pressures they both had to deal with, and that the result, quite naturally, is that their relationship has suffered. It is therefore the relationship that is in need of TLC (tender loving care or nurturing), rather than the individuals needing correction. By getting people to focus on improving the relationship I am asking them to look outside themselves and giving them something to do that does not threaten them.

Look for what is working

We can quickly become obsessed with problems and failure. Looking for contribution can also ask about what is working. It is far easier to build on something that works than to fix something that is broken. A vital stepping stone which helps people quickly move past recrimination and blame is to ask about successes and times when the difficult behaviour has not occurred or has not been a hindrance. Once we have introduced the notion that something is working the mood can quickly start to change and a more productive working relationship will ensue. We are not out of the woods yet but heading in the right direction. When things are not going right for us our negative view can start to colour everything. It might be that only 5 per cent of our working day is not working for us, but we'll start to believe the whole job is rotten unless we challenge it with a few balancing thoughts. Similarly, people will quickly focus on the small percentage of a relationship that is not going too well and completely ignore the fact that large parts of it function without any problem. Identifying the positive elements and the times when things are working well is intended to redress the balance and offer new possibilities.

Ask the Miracle Question

The Miracle Question is a device taken from the field of Solution Focused work[4]. 'Solution focused' means looking for successful outcomes (solutions) rather than focusing on problems. The question to ask is:

'Imagine that tonight, while you are asleep, a miracle happens which means that the (obstacle or problem) we are discussing goes away. As you have been asleep, you will be unaware of the Miracle and its effects, but when you awaken in the morning things will be different. How will you know that the miracle has occurred?'

In asking this question – either of ourselves or others – the aim is to elicit information about how life/work/the relationship or whatever will be after the problem has gone away. The Miracle Question is a device to enable the person of whom it is asked to move beyond their present, problem-saturated state of mind and imagine how things will be post-problem. The aim is to gather information about what they will be doing when they are free of the constraints of the problem. The emphasis is on their behaviour (rather than their thoughts or feelings). It is a question that requires a certain degree of persistence, but which yields great results when used skilfully. The trick is to build as rich an image as possible of a world where the problem has vanished and the kind of differences it will make in that person's life.

From here it is possible to start to develop goals. Many people find this slightly unnatural (we have been so conditioned to believe that the answer lies in studying the problem). However, when they start working towards where they want to go despite the problem, they usually find that it starts to diminish its hold over them.

Plan your actions

Agree on who does what, and then start to do it. Decide on the main areas of responsibility and what contribution each participant will make. Maintain contact by deciding in advance when the next meeting will be. Do not let too much time pass between meetings until you are confident that things are running better. I usually suggest two or three days to a week in the early stages. Also, agree how you will know that progress is happening. This can then be checked and built on during follow-up meetings. Avoid the temptation to drop back into 'problem talk' – stay focused on what has been working since the last meeting. If problems or setbacks have occurred, frame them as something to be tackled collaboratively ('How are *we* going to handle this?').

What could go wrong?

A final question here is 'What could go wrong?' This allows you both (or both parties if you are mediating) to troubleshoot the project *before* any obstacles arise. It asks the participants to think ahead, mentally working through their plan. Any possible pitfalls can then be prepared for by developing a Plan B. For example, in one organisation I met two staff members trying to resolve a conflict and work more productively together. When one of them was asked the question 'What could go wrong?' she replied 'She might start gossiping about me again'. The other person protested that she wouldn't, and we told her that we knew she meant it, but suggested that misunderstandings might still arise and that since there was quite clearly a 'gossip mill' in the company she might even get falsely accused. This allowed both parties to forward plan by agreeing that, in the event of any suggestions that the colleague had gossiped, both parties could talk about it together before reacting and call us if they needed help to resolve any misunderstandings.

The ideas included in this chapter can help get you 'unstuck' if you are not sure how to proceed with a difficult person. In order to become more familiar with the tactics, my advice is not to wait until a difficult situation crops up but to practise some of them in your day-to-day dealings with others. In fact I would recommend this for any of the tactics mentioned in the book, because the skills needed for dealing with challenging situations are merely an extension of those we should be using elsewhere in our lives. Regular practice will mean they'll soon become a part of your interpersonal repertoire and you'll be able to call on them without a second thought.

Conclusion

Human relationships can provoke a bewildering, unpredictable and seemingly erratic range of responses from the people living in them. Given the complexity of our interactions and the risk of failure – coupled with the fundamental truth that we have to get along in groups or die out – you would expect our millennia-long history of social development and thousands of years of civilisation to have produced more in the way of sound advice on how to live together.

The active suggestions contained in this book, however, provide a pretty fair toolkit for dealing with almost any type of difficult situation, and have been shown to improve outcomes in getting round difficult people. I am sure you will be able to add some of your own skills to use in certain situations.

It has often been said that if there are over 60 million people in the United Kingdom then there are over 60 million ways of being difficult. Given the infinite variety of possible combinations of difficult behaviour, you will certainly come up against people who don't fit neatly into any of the seven categories I have described and it may be hard to identify exactly what is 'difficult' about them. Perhaps they mix two or three different behaviours or camouflage their obstructiveness, or their behaviour is so subtle it takes months or even years to see just what is going on.

Whatever the difficult person is doing – no matter how serious or urgent the consequences – there is no 'silver bullet' or sure-fire approach to dealing with them. Some people will respond quickly and favourably to a direct appeal about their behaviour, some will deny that there is a problem and others will accept that there is, but refuse to take any responsibility for helping to solve it. In all cases it is worth seeing the behaviour as a product of the relationship and the context in which it occurs. You need to decide what sort of outcome you want and then work towards that goal. This will be more productive than looking for blame or trying to decide who is at fault.

The range of abilities required for dealing with difficult behaviour come under the broad heading of interpersonal skills which, as well as involving how we interact with others, also include how we respond ourselves – how we observe and handle our thoughts, feelings, attitudes and behaviour. The more we practise and the greater our sincerity in improving these skills, the more successful our outcomes are likely to be. We can't win 'em all as they say, so it is reassuring to know that greater self-awareness also helps take the sting out of our inevitable 'failures'. Moreover, we need to keep our skills in good fettle. If we don't use them, we'll lose them.

It is worth reflecting on the fact that any one of us, even the most inept among us, has more successes than failures in our daily interactions. Of the literally thousands of communications that we will have each week, only very few break down or are difficult. It can be a real resource to realise that we already have all the skills we need, even though we may not be using them in the right place or at the right time. For example, many people tell me that they can handle other people's strident and argumentative behaviour better when they are at work than when they are at home; when they have their 'professional' hat on they are more in control, or vice versa. In other words, they already have the skills they need, they simply (or not so simply) need to be able to use them in a different situation.

A successful outcome

Jodie was a nurse in a centre for people with mental health problems. She took over the role of the 'named nurse' for a young woman with mild learning disabilities who – with a complex history of mental ill health – had been in residential care for nine years. The patient had never found these placements satisfactory and had often complained of ill-treatment. The situation was complicated by her parents' involvement. Naturally protective of their daughter they had frequently intervened on her behalf and, when Jodie stepped into her new position, the relationship was already complicated by the parents' mistrust and general negativity 'towards the services as a whole'.[1] Neither the patient nor her parents thought that their complaints had ever been taken seriously or handled well. The result was that the father frequently became confrontational, was generally defensive and unhelpful and often caused trouble which not only tied up staff, it also upset them – so much so that he was known to be difficult by all the staff, whether they had been directly involved with him or not.

'I was aware of the previous conflicts,' said Jodie, 'though I had never been involved in or witnessed one of his outbursts. The first time I met the father he was very, very angry and immediately demanded to see the person in charge (which was me). Just as well really, since all my colleagues were suddenly very busy elsewhere!

'I greeted him calmly and confidently and offered my hand in greeting. We shook hands and I asked him if he would like to go somewhere less public for a quiet chat. I took him to one of the centre's sitting rooms where I sat down and listened, giving him my full attention. Once he had finished his account (which took about 10 minutes, but seemed much longer) I acknowledged what I had heard without attempting to explain or excuse any of the complaints he had raised. I also explained my role as his daughter's new home nurse and main contact person and gave him details of my shifts so that he would know my availability should he need me. I said that I would look into his concerns, taking care not to promise anything we could not deliver, and asked him if he would like to meet again.

'We arranged to speak again the following week and when we did he was already less confrontational. He explained that he and his wife had never felt listened to, and that their insights into their daughter's behaviour and needs had never been valued. As a result we agreed that, in future, I would consult them if I needed information about their daughter – she also agreed with this.

'At each meeting we would set a date for the next. This meant that we had regular contact rather than only meeting when there was a crisis. After a few weeks these discussions became very positive. They provided support for the father and helped his daughter as she began to notice his attitude towards the system changing. Conflict still arose from time to time but now we had a framework for dealing with it; I was always careful to listen calmly and responded by telling him how we were dealing with his daughter's case and what action I would be taking in response to his concerns. Despite this, there were times when he made claims that, frankly, seemed untrue. I felt confident to challenge him, when necessary, without damaging our positive relationship.'

Jodie finished her account by telling me that the positive relationship with the father continued beyond his daughter's discharge from the unit and transfer to another one. 'When the daughter left us there was sincere understanding on both sides. In fact I continued to act as an advocate for the parents in meetings that they were concerned about or which they found difficult.'

This true story about a man who was seen as persistently difficult serves as a reminder that the ability to handle such a situation relies on a genuine wish to work things out and qualities such as sincerity, patience and empathy. The quality of the relationship is paramount; Jodie sought first to understand the man's predicament, listening to his views and letting him voice his concerns without seeing them as an attack. She was then able to work with him collaboratively on their common interest – what really mattered was his daughter's welfare.

I have heard of hundreds of such stories. Some of them were undoubtedly life changing, such as the one above, but many more were the small, seemingly insignificant successes that we so frequently overlook. Often these have come to light during my workshops and seminars where, away from the demands of the job for a day, people have time to reflect on their work. It is at such moments that we can identify our successes,[2] which, as I have said before, are far more common than we realise. When we realise this it can give us the energy we need for problem-solving, drawing on resources we had forgotten we had.

In thinking about the ideas I have proposed in this book, remember to plan your strategy in advance. Practise before you need it and you'll start to find that you can turn difficult situations into manageable ones. Keep in mind that what we want out of these approaches is not to get the other person to change. We just want to move things forward despite their awkward behaviour. And the best thing is – the cause of the problem, the difficult person – won't even realise that their difficult behaviour has been successfully handled.

Notes

Chapter 1

1. *People Skills: How to Assert Yourself, Listen to Others and Resolve Conflicts,* R Bolton, Simon and Schuster, 1979.
2. 'Social Workers are Sick Leave Champions', T Robbins and D Brown, *Sunday Times,* 24 June 2001.
3. *Stress and Low Morale are the Hidden Costs of the UK's £13 billion Absenteeism Bill,* Industrial Society, 7 February 2000.
4. *Grooming, Gossip and the Evolution of Language,* R Dunbar, Faber & Faber, 1996.
5. *Montaillon,* E Le Roy Ladurie, Vintage, New York, 1979.
6. *Relating to Others,* Steve Duck, Open University Press, 1999.
7. 'Who are Nurses? What Do Nurses Do?', Peter Burgess in *Nursing Times,* 23 May 2001.
8. 'Social Workers are Sick Leave Champions', op.cit.
9. *Confronting Company Politics,* Beverley Stone, Macmillan Press, 1999.

Chapter 2

1. *Civility, Manners, Morals and the Etiquette of Democracy,* S Carter, Basic Books, 1998.
2. The Prediction of Violence in a Health Care Setting, in *Violence and health care professionals,* R Whittington & T Wykes, Chapman and Hall, 1994.
3. 'Children's Behaviour Worse, Say Teachers', Liz Lightfoot in the *Daily Telegraph,* 2 September 2001.
4. *192 million Days Lost to Absence,* CBI Survey, 15 May 2001.
5. Carried out on behalf of the GMB union by Glasgow University Health and Safety Research Team, N Daly, *Nursing Times,* 6 December 2000.
6. 'Benefits of Harnessing Conflict in the Office', *Sunday Times,* 24 June 2001.
7. *Living Well, the Psychology of Everyday Life,* M Csikzentmihaly, Weidenfield & Nicolson, 1997.

8. *Is the UK Moving Up the International Wellbeing Rankings?* DG Blanchflower and AJ Oswald, May 2000, available on the University of Warwick website: http://www.oswald.co.uk
9. *Hand-Me-Down-Blues,* Michael Yapko, St. Martin's Press, 1999.
10. *Clinical Handbook of Marital and Couples Intervention,* K Halford & H Markman, Wiley, 1997.
11. *The Marriage Clinic, a Scientifically Based Marital Therapy,* J M Gottman, WW Norton, 1999.
12. *Clinical Handbook of Marital and Couples Intervention,* op.cit.
13. *Adult Bullying: Perpetrators and Victims,* P Randall, Routledge, 1997.

Chapter 3

1. The subject of rules in relationships is a huge topic and one which many people have found helpful when struggling with difficult relationships. If you want to know more on the subject I suggest you read Virgina Satir's *The New Peoplemaking,* Science and Behaviour Books, 1988.
2. This phrase – which dates from a time when people where not so careful about their use of language – refers to the idea that people locked into a dispute are often unable to hear each other. It is not intended as a reflection on how deaf people or those with impaired hearing communicate.
3. See *Emotional Intelligence* by Daniel Goleman, Bloomsbury, 1996 for more on what he calls 'emotional hijacking'.
4. *Christmas Truce,* M Brown & S Seaton, Pan, 1999.
5. *The Heart of Conflict,* Brian Muldoon, GP Putnam's Sons, New York, 1996

Chapter 4

1. *Emotional Intelligence,* Daniel Goleman, Bloomsbury, 1996.
2. *The Emotional Brain: the Mysterious Underpinnings of Emotional Life,* Joseph LeDoux, Touchstone, 1996.
3. For more on the perplexing question of 'Why?' see *Change, Principles of Problem Formation and Problem Resolution,* Watzlawick, et al.
4. *Change, Principles of Problem Formation and Problem Resolution,* Watzlawick, Weakland and Fisch, WW Norton, 1974.
5. *Hair Brain, Tortoise Mind,* Guy Claxton, Fourth Estate, 1997.

6. Reported in the *Sunday Times,* 18 July 1976.

7. *Virginibus Puerisque,* Robert Louis Stevenson, 1881.

8. Such a statement does not do justice to one of the most exciting periods of scientific development in the history of humankind, which occurred during the second half of the nineteenth century. The first institute of experimental psychology was opened in Leipzig in 1879 by Wilhelm Wund. Wund was building on the inspired contribution of German physician and philosopher Gustav Fechner. In what he termed his 'psychophysical law', Fechner attempted to unite the physical and the spiritual worlds and provided one of the cornerstones of the new discipline of psychology. Freud later borrowed several of Fechner's propositions and incorporated them into his metapsychology. See *The Discovery of the Unconscious* by Henry Ellenberger for more a complete description.

9. After publication of the *Principles* James lost all interest in psychology describing it as a 'nasty little subject; all one cares to know lies outside it.'

10. *Plato not Prozac, Applying Philosophy to Everyday Problems,* Lou Marinoff, Harper Collins, 1999.

11. I am not for a moment suggesting meek submission to insulting behaviour. Some situations cannot be changed or some people may feel unable or unwilling to tackle them immediately. This question then comes into its own.

12. *Deductive Criminal Profiling: Comparing Applied Methodologies between Inductive and Deductive Profiling Techniques,* Brent E. Turvey, MS, 1998 Knowledge Solutions Library, Electronic Publication, URL: http://www.corpus-delicti.com/Profiling_law.html

13. *Language in Thought and Action* (5th edition), SI and R Hayakawa, Harcourt, Brace, Jovanovich, 1990.

Chapter 5

1. *Nature's Mind: the Biological Roots of Thinking, Emotions, Sexuality, Language and Intelligence,* Michael Gazzaniga, Penguin Books, 1994.

2. *Emotional Intelligence,* Daniel Goleman, Bloomsbury, 1996.

3. *Why Zebras Don't get Ulcers: an Updated Guide to Stress, Stress Related Diseases and Coping,* Robert Sapolsky, W H Freeman & Company, 1998.

4. Terms like 'the stress bandwagon', 'malingering' and 'swinging the lead' are typical of the comments I have heard in relation to work-related stress.

5. Of course, some individuals and responsible employers do take the

matter seriously with stress reduction programmes. These too, however, are generally aimed at the physical manifestations of stress, with the emotional consequences as a by-product. Little currency is given to the idea that people under stress perform less well emotionally and cognitively.

6. *Why Zebras Don't get Ulcers: an Updated Guide to Stress, Stress Related Diseases and Coping,* op.cit.

7. Sapolsky also takes care to point out that it is not simply being low down in a social hierarchy that means high levels of stress. Subordinate animals suffer most from stress-related diseases where their low status is accompanied by 'lots of harassment and high costs for cheating'. *Why Zebras Don't get Ulcers: an Updated Guide to Stress, Stress Related Diseases and Coping,* op.cit.

8. *Unhealthy Societies: the Afflictions of Inequality,* Richard Wilkinson, Routledge, 1996.

9. Low Job Control and Risk of Coronary Heart Disease in Whitehall II (Prospective Cohort) Study, Hans Bosma et al, *BMJ,* 22 February 1997.

10. The risk is not linked to the employment grade, the demands of the job or the degree of social support at work. It is the real or perceived sense of control that is the decisive factor.

11. Kiecolt-Glaser's research is cited in *The Sickening Mind: Brain, Behaviour, Immunity and Disease,* Paul Martin, Harper Collins, 1997.

12. 'Long-Term Caregiving: What Happens When it Ends?' S Robinson-Whelan et al, *Journal of Abnormal Psychology,* November 2001.

13. 'Protective and Damaging Effects of Stress Mediators', Bruce McEwen, *New England Journal of Medicine,* 338(3) 1998.

14. *Why Zebras Don't get Ulcers: an Updated Guide to Stress, Stress Related Diseases and Coping,* op.cit.

15. *Mapping the Mind,* Rita Carter, Weidenfeld and Nicolson, 1998.

16. *Mind-Body Medicine: a Clinician's Guide to Psychoneuroimmunology,* Alan Watkins (ed), Churchill Livingstone, 1997.

17. *Why Zebras Don't get Ulcers: an Updated Guide to Stress, Stress Related Diseases and Coping,* op.cit.

18. 'Protective and Damaging Effects of Stress Mediators', op.cit.

19. *The Emotional Brain: the Mysterious Underpinnings of Emotional Life,* Joseph LeDoux, Touchstone, 1996.

20. *Social Cognition: Making Sense of People,* Ziva Kunda, MIT Press, 1999.

21. *The Psychology of Interpersonal Behaviour,* Michael Argyle, Penguin, 1994 (5th edition).

22. *The Origin of Everyday Moods: Managing Energy, Tension and Stress,* Robert Thayer, Oxford University Press, 1996.

23. *The Emotional Brain,* op. cit.

24. *Emotional Intelligence,* op. cit.

25. *Mind the Gap: Hierarchies, Health and Human Evolution,* Richard Wilkinson, Weidenfeld and Nicolson, 2000.

26. *The New Peoplemaking,* Virginia Satir, Science and Behavior Books 1988.

27. *The New Peoplemaking,* op. cit.

28. Or, felt good about themselves. 'In control' here means in control of their feelings rather than mastery over the situation.

29. Typical stances taken by people in negotiations are that they: (1) Retaliate in a like manner (Blaming); (2) Capitulate to appease other party (Placating); (3) Ignore the problem in an attempt to eliminate it (Computing); (4) Deviate by changing the subject (Distracting). See *Getting Past No: Negotiating with Difficult People,* William Ury, Century Business Books, 1991.

30. *Silent Messages: Implicit Communication of Emotions and Attitudes,* Albert Mehrabian, Wadsworth Publishing, 1981 (2nd edition).

31. *Divided Labours: an Evolutionary View of Women at Work,* Kingsley Brown, Weidenfeld and Nicolson, 1998.

32. *You Just Don't Understand: Women and Men in Conversation,* Deborah Tannen, William Morrow and Co, 1990. (Now available from Virago in the UK)

33. *War of Words: Women and Men Arguing,* Elizabeth Mapstone, Chatto and Windus, 1998.

34. *Why Marriages Succeed or Fail: and How You Can Make Yours Last,* John Gottman, Bloomsbury, 1997.

35. *War of Words,* op. cit.

36. John Gottman and his colleagues at the University of Washington have done over 20 years' research into the communication styles of couples. When interviewing stonewallers (usually, but not always men), he says that they 'often claim that they are trying to be neutral' and that they do not realise how the behaviour can worsen the situation.

37. *Talking from 9 to 5: How Women's and Men's Conversational Styles Affect Who Gets Heard,* Deborah Tannen, Virago, 1994.

38. *War of Words,* op. cit.

39. 'Marital Discord and Depression: Two Major Social Problems', Hyman Hops et al. In *Clinical Handbook of Marriage and Couples Interventions,* K Halford and H Markman (eds), Wiley & Sons, 1997.

40. *Clinical Handbook of Marriage and Couples Intervention,* op. cit.

41. 'Biobehavioral Responses to Stress in Females: Tend-and-Befriend, not Fight-or-Flight', Shelley Taylor et al, *Psychological Review,* 107(3), July 2000.

42. *The New Science of Intimate Relationships*, Garth Fletcher, Blackwell Publishing, 2002.
43. This, as I have found out during my seminars and workshops, can be a contentious issue. I am not denying the importance of feelings, I am saying that the acknowledgement of feelings is vital to the process, but exploring them when in the middle of a difficult encounter can be unhelpful and might provoke defensiveness in the other person.

Chapter 6

1. It was Yogi Berra, the renowned American baseball player, who said this. His many witty and sharp aphorisms, though at first sight slightly inept ('You can observe a lot just by watching') and even self-incriminating ('The towels were so thick there I could hardly close my suitcase'), had the unerring knack of capturing the sense of the moment and conveying something beyond their apparent throwaway nature - which is probably why they are so often quoted today.
2. This can be an area of confusion for both staff and managers. I have often met experienced staff who either ignore the protocols which are there to protect them or do not know that they exist. Organisations should not assume that because a code of working practice has been drawn up that everyone knows about it or knows how to apply it.
3. *War of Words, Women and Men Arguing*, Elizabeth Mapstone, Chatto and Windus, 1998.
4. *Social Skills at Work,* David Fontana, British Psychological Society, 1990.

Chapter 7

1. *How to Disagree without Being Disagreeable: Getting your Point Across,* S Haden Elgin, John Wiley, 1997.
2. *Ericksonian Approaches, a Comprehensive Manual,* R Battino and TL South, Crown House Publishing, 1999.
3. *The Magic of Rapport,* Jerry Richardson, Meta Publications, California, 1987.
4. I am often asked about matching the behaviour of hostile or aggressive people. My reply is that the aim is to match the physical stance and rhythm and pitch of the voice, not the hostility or the aggression. Quite clearly we do not want to mirror threats or finger-wagging. If in doubt, don't do it at all.

5. *Silent Messages: Implicit Communication of Emotions and Attitudes*, Albert Mehrabian, Wadsworth Publishing, 1981 (2nd edition).

6. Verbal communication, that is to say language, is a relatively recent phenomenon in terms of human evolution. The 'instinct' or 'gut feelings' we often speak about are often informed by the non-verbal communications of our early ancestors, which was all they had to rely on. These are skills we too possess even though we often ignore them, and they feature in every human interaction.

Chapter 8

1. Or PTSD for short. Symptoms include involuntary recall of the traumatic event, flashbacks, nightmares and a number of other troubling effects, as the sufferer does not just remember the cause of the trauma, they actually experience the full emotional response as though re-living the event.

2. The objection here is often raised that if we apologise we admit culpability. In other words, 'sorry' equals guilt. I do not agree with this. In fact, I think such an attitude is positively harmful. We all want an apology when we feel we have been wronged, it acknowledges our distress. Notice how large public bodies like NHS trusts, churches and even governments now issue a standard statement along the lines of 'First let us say how deeply sorry we are that...' whenever there is a high-profile complaint made against them.

3. This is, of course, a gender stereotype. Not all men use jibes and banter in this way and some women are very effective at it. Deborah Tannen refers to this sort of ritualised opposition as Agonism. See *The Argument Culture: Moving from Debate to Dialogue,* Deborah Tannen, Random House, 1998.

Chapter 10

1. *A Couple's Guide to Communication,* J Gottman, et al. Research Press, 1976.

2. John Gottman (personal communication)

3. *Difficult Conversations, How to Discuss what Matters Most,* D Stone, B Patton, S Heen, Michael Joseph, 1999.

4. *The Solutions Focus, the Simple Way to Positive Change*, P Jackson, M McKergow, Nicholas Brealey Publishing, 2002. This is a good guide to using Solution Focused techniques in organisations. There is also a rich

and readable literature on SFBT (Solution Focused Brief Therapy); publishers Norton and Sage have many of the best titles. Both lists can be viewed on the internet. A few recommended titles are also listed in the Principal References at the end of this book.

Conclusion

1. Jodie (not her real name) wrote this report for me so I am quoting her here.
2. *Hare Brain Tortoise Mind: Why Intelligence Increases when You Think Less*, Guy Claxton, Fourth Estate, 1997.

Principal References

Argyle, Michael, *The Psychology of Interpersonal Behaviour*, 5th edn., Penguin, London, 1990.

Birtchnell, John, *How Humans Relate: a New Interpersonal Theory*, Psychology Press, Hove, 1993.

Bosma, H. et al. Low Job Control and Risk of Coronary Heart Disease in Whitehall II (Prospective Cohort) Study, *British Medical Journal*, 22 February, 1997.

Bostrom, Robert, *Listening Behaviour, Measurement and Application*, The Guilford Press, New York, 1990.

Brody, Leslie, *Gender, Emotion and the Family*, Harvard University Press, Cambridge, Mass., 1999.

Browne, K., *Divided Labours: an Evolutionary View of Women at Work*, Weidenfeld & Nicolson, London, 1998.

Carter, Rita, *Mapping the Mind*, Weidenfeld & Nicolson, London, 1998.

Carter, Stephen, L., *Civility, Manners Morals and the Etiquette of Democracy*, Basic Books, New York, 1998.

Claxton, Guy, *Hare Brain Tortoise Mind, Why Intelligence Increases When You Think Less*, Fourth Estate, London, 1997.

Dimitrius, J., Mazzarella, M. (1998). *Reading People*, Vermilion, London, 1998.

Dunbar, Robin, *Grooming, Gossip and the Evolution of Language*, Faber & Faber, London, 1996.

Eckman, Paul, *Telling Lies, Clues to Deceit in the Marketplace, Politics and Marriage*, WW Norton & Co, New York, 2001.

Ellenberger, Henri, *The Discovery of the Unconscious*, Basic Books, New York, 1970.

Evans, S. and Suib Cohen, S., *Hot Buttons, How to Resolve Conflict and Cool Everyone Down*, Piatkus, London, 2000.

Fletcher, Garth, *The New Science of Intimate Relationships*, Blackwell, 2002.

Gallois, C., Callan, V., *Communication and Culture*, a Guide for Practice, John Wiley & Sons, Chichester, 1997.

Gazzaniga Michael, *Nature's Mind: the Biological Roots of Thinking, Emotions, Sexuality, Language and Intelligence*, Penguin, London, 1992.

Goleman, Daniel, *Emotional Intelligence*, Bloomsbury, London 1996.

Gottman, J.M., and Silver, N., *Why Marriages Succeed or Fail*, Bloomsbury, London, 1997.

Gottman, J.M., Notarius, C., Gonso, G., & Markman, H., *A Couple's Guide to Communication*, Research Press, Champaign, 1976.

Gottman, J.M., *What Predicts Divorce?* Lawrence Erlbaum Associates, Hillsdale, 1994.

Haden Elgin, Suzette, *How to Disagree Without Being Disagreeable*, John Wiley & Sons, New York, 1997.

Halford, K., and Markman, H., (Eds.), *Clinical Handbook of Marriage and Couples Interventions*, John Wiley & Sons, Chichester, 1997.

Hare, Robert, *Without Conscience: the Disturbing World of the Psychopaths Among Us*, The Guilford Press, New York, 1993.

Hargie, Owen, (Ed.), *The Handbook of Communication Skills*, Routledge. London 1997.

Kunda, Ziva, *Social Cognition, Making Sense of People*, MIT Press, Cambridge, Mass., 1999.

LeDoux, Joseph, *The Emotional Brain: the Mysterious Underpinnings of Emotional Life*, Simon & Schuster, New York, 1996.

Mapstone, Elizabeth, *War of Words: Women and Men Arguing*, Chatto & Windus, London, 1998.

Marinoff, Lou, *Plato Not Prozac: Applying Philosophy to Everyday Problems*, Harper Collins, New York, 1999.

Martin, Paul, *The Sickening Mind: Brain, Behaviour, Immunity and Disease*, Harper Collins, London, 1997.

McEwen, Bruce, Protective and Damaging Effects of Stress Mediators, *New England Journal of Medicine*, 338(3) 1998.

Mehrabian, Albert, *Silent Messages: Implicit Communication of Emotions and Attitudes*, Wadsworth, Inc., Belmont, 1981.

Muldoon, Brian, *The Heart of Conflict*, G.P. Putnam's Sons, New York, 1996.

Pease, A. & B., *Why Men Don't Listen and Women Can't Read Maps*, Orion Publishing Group, London, 1999.

Pinker, Steven, *How the Mind Works*, Penguin, London, 1997.

Randall, Peter, *Adult Bullying: Perpetrators and Victims*, Routledge, London, 1997.

Rich Harris, Judith, *The Nurture Assumption, Why Children Turn Out the Way They Do*, Bloomsbury, London, 1998.

Richardson, Jerry, *The Magic of Rapport: How You Can Gain Personal Power in Any Situation*, Meta Publications, Capitola, 1987.

Robinson-Whelan, S., et al. 'Long-term Caregiving: What Happens When it Ends?' *Journal of Abnormal Psychology*, November 2001.

Sapolsky, Robert, *Why Zebras Don't Get Ulcers, an Updated Guide to Stress, Stress Related Diseases and Coping*, WH Freeman & Co, New York, 1998.

Satir, Virginia, *The New Peoplemaking*, Science and Behavior Books, Mountain View, 1988.

Stone, D., Patton, B., & Heen, S., *Difficult Conversations: How to Discuss what Matters Most*, Michael Joseph, London, 1999.

Swann, Christine. 'Public Health and the Gendered Body', *The Psychologist*, Vol. 15 No. 4, July 2002.

Tannen, Deborah, *Talking from 9 to 5, How Women's and Man's Conversational Styles Affect Who Gets Heard*, Virago, London, 1995.

Tannen, Deborah, *The Argument Culture, Moving from Debate to Dialogue*, Random House, New York, 1998.

Tannen, Deborah, *You Just Don't Understand: Women and Men in Conversation*, Wm. Morrow & Co, New York, 1990.

Taylor, S. et al., 'Biobehavioral Responses to Stress in Females: Tend-and-Befriend, not Fight-or-Flight'. *Psychological Review*, 107 (3), July, 2000.

Thayer, Robert, *The Origin of Everyday Moods, Managing Energy, Tension and Stress*, Oxford University Press, New York, 1996.

Ury, William, *Getting Past No, Negotiating with Difficult People*, Century Business Books, London, 1991.

Watkins, Alan, (Ed.), *Mind-Body Medicine, a Clinician's Guide to Psychoneuroimmunology*, Churchill Livingstone, New York, 1997.

Watzlawick, P., Weakland, J., and Fisch, R., *Change, Principles of Problem Formation and Problem Resolution*, WW Norton, New York, 1974.

Wilkinson, Richard, *Mind the Gap: Hierarchies, Health and Human Evolution*, Weidenfeld & Nicolson, London, 2000.

Wilkinson, Richard, *Unhealthy Societies, the Afflictions of Inequality*, Routledge, London, 1996.

Yapko, Michael, *Hand-Me-Down-Blues, How to Stop Depression From Spreading in Families*, St. Martin's Press, New York, 1999.

Index

Neill, Dr Sean 30
Niebuhr, Reinhold 45
nurses 15
Nursing Times 15

objective, remaining 110-112, 183, 190
observations 59, 62, 75
offender profiling 62
open questions 168
Oswald, Professor Andrew 34

paralysis by analysis 59
perceptions, effects on physiology 90
personal safety 22-23
pessimism 35
'Placater, the' 92-94
point scoring 44
post-traumatic stress disorder (PTSD) 88, 126
'Principles of Psychology' 60
psychological research 19

questions, open and closed 168

Race Relations Act 41
rapport
  building 119-124, 173
  talk 99
regret, expressing 192
relationship maintenance 12
remaining objective 110-112, 183, 190
report talk 99
resources, for personal relationships 19
risk assessment 56
Roosevelt, Eleanor 41, 187

SALVAGE strategy 186-188
Sapolsky, Robert 83
Satir, Virginia 91-94
self-respect 48
Selye, Hans 78
Serenity prayer 45
setting boundaries 109-110
Sex Discrimination Act 41
'Shadow, the' 159-167
Shaw, George Bernard 100
short-term gain 52-54
'Silent Type, the' 167
skills, lack of 70
social hierarchy and stress 83-84
Solution Focused work 199
staying cool 110-112
'Steamroller, the' 127-135
Stevenson, Robert Louis 60
Stockdale, Sue 77
Stone, Patton and Heen 197
stress
  chronic 82-85
  effect on memory 87-88
  effect on mood 88
  effects of 71
  effects on thinking 85-87
  and gender 97-100
  good and bad 78
  management 83
  physiological changes during 81
  and social hierarchy 83-84
  in the workplace 84
stress-induced behaviour 70
stressors in the workplace 80
Sunday Times 11

Tannen, Deborah 97, 99, 101
Thayer, Robert 88